Using and Understanding Maps

The Endangered World

Consulting Editor
Scott E. Morris
College of Mines and Earth Resources
University of Idaho

Chelsea House Publishers
New York   Philadelphia

This Publication was designed, edited and computer generated by
Lovell Johns Limited
10 Hanborough Business Park
Long Hanborough
Witney
Oxon, England OX8 8LH

The contents of this volume are based on the latest data available at the
time of publication.

Map credit: *Antarctica source map prepared at 1:20,000 by the British
Antarctic Survey Mapping and Geographic Information Centre, 1990.*

Cover credit: *Reuters/Bettman*

Printed in Mexico

First printing

1 3 5 7 9 8 6 4 2

Library of Congress Cataloging in Publication Data

The Endangered world/editorial consultant, Scott Morris:
      p. cm. (Using and understanding maps)
      Includes glossary and index/gazetteer.
      Includes bibliographical references.
      Summary: Eighteen map spreads highlight the damage pollution
      has done to our world.
      ISBN 0-7910-1806-7. ISBN 0-7910-1819-9 (pbk.)
1. Man — Influence on nature — Maps.
[1. Pollution — Maps. 2. Atlases.]
      I. Morris. Scott Edward. II. Chelsea House Publishers. III. Series.
      G1046.E1E5 1993 <G&M>
      363.7' 0022' 3 — dc20   92-22289
                                                 CIP
                                                 MAP AC

Introduction

We inhabit a fascinating and mysterious planet where the earth's physical features, life-forms, and the diversity of human culture conspire to produce a breathtaking environment. We don't have to travel very far to see and experience the wealth of this diverse planet; in fact, we don't have to travel at all. Everywhere images of the world are abundantly available in books, newspapers, magazines, movies, television, and the arts. We could say that *everywhere* one looks, our world is a brilliant moving tapestry of shapes, colors, and textures, and our experience of its many messages — whether in our travels or simply by gazing out into our own backyards — is what we call reality.

Geography is the study of a portion of that reality. More so, it is the study of how the physical and biological components (rocks, animals, plants, and people) of our planet are distributed and how they are interconnected. Geographers seek to describe and to explain the physical patterns that have evolved on the earth and also to discover the significance in the ways they have evolved. To do this, geographers rely on maps.

Maps can be powerful images. They convey selective information about vast areas of an overwhelmingly cluttered world. The cartographer, or mapmaker, must carefully choose the theme of a map, that is, what it will show, knowing that a good map will convey the essence of information while at the same time making the information easy to comprehend.

This volume and its companions in UNDERSTANDING AND USING MAPS are about the planet we call earth and the maps we use to find our way along its peaks and valleys. Each volume displays map images that reveal how the world is arranged according to a specific theme such as population, industries or the endangered world. The maps in each volume are accompanied by an interesting collection of facts — some are rather obvious, others are oddities. Yet all are meant to be informative.

Along with a wealth of facts, there are explanations of the various attributes and phenomena depicted by the maps. This information is provided to better understand the significance of the maps as well as to demonstrate how the many themes relate.

Names for places are essential to geographers. To study the world without devising names for places would be extremely difficult. But geographers also know that names are in no way permanent; place names change as people change. The recent reunification of Germany and the breakup of what was the Soviet Union — events that seem colossal from the perspective of socioeconomics — to geographers are simply events that require the drawing or erasing of one or a few boundaries and the renaming of one or several land masses. The geographer is constantly reminded that the world is in flux; a map is always in danger of being rendered obsolete by a turn in current events.

Because the world is dynamic, it continues to captivate the mind and stimulate the imagination. USING AND UNDERSTANDING MAPS presents the world as it is today, with the reservation that any dramatic rearrangement of land and people is likely, indeed inevitable, thus requiring the making of a new map. In this way maps are themselves a part of the evolutionary process.

Scott E. Morris

The Endangered World

The world's population has doubled in the last 40 years; there are now more than 5.2 billion people on the earth. These people need land to live on, and natural resources are required to support them. But the development of these resources for humankind has resulted in environmental pollution and the destruction of habitat for other plant and animal species. Consequently, large areas of our world are endangered.

Before the onset of the 20th century, the impact of human civilization on the landscape was localized. Pollution existed, ecosystems were modified or even destroyed, and some life-forms were undoubtedly extinguished, but the damage done was negligible compared to what has occurred since the advent of modern machinery.

In the 20th century we have dramatically affected our planet and the ecosystems it supports. The ability of modern equipment to alter the landscape with ease, combined with increasing population and the associated surge in the use of our planet's resources, has resulted in a change not only in the landscape but in the composition of our atmosphere. This process will in all likelihood change the climates of the earth.

The expansion of human population into areas that were until recently wildland has resulted in the loss of habitat for animal and plant species. As a result, species that once thrived are now endangered, and many face extinction. Reliable estimates suggest that the world is losing roughly 100 species per day. Some endangered species are well known — the elephant, rhinoceros, and mountain gorilla of Africa; the tiger in India, the panda in China — others, including most of the endangered plant species, are unfamilar to most people. But every species is part of the planet's ecological balance.

Saving the endangered world must be a priority, for both moral and biological reasons. Not only must we respect the inherent right of every species to exist; there are also benefits to humankind from healthy, diverse ecosystems. Many wild areas serve as watersheds, supplying clean water to cities and towns. Plants especially are a large untapped resource that has a direct impact on the "health" of the human race. Plants serve not only as our primary food supply; they are an important source of medicinal products.

Additionally, and perhaps most important, all organisms are part of the earth's ecosystem. We are just beginning to understand how intricately the web of life is connected to the very health of the planet. In this context, we can see how deforestation of large land areas may influence the climate of distant places; how air and water pollution in one country can and does pollute the environment in others; how automobile traffic and power generation in the developed nations alter the chemistry of the world's atmosphere. Many scientists estimate that global temperatures will rise in the next century. There is no way of predicting all the consequences of such a change, but they are bound to be far-reaching.

There is hope. In June 1992, world leaders met in Rio de Janeiro for the first Earth Summit — a global effort to formulate policies for addressing the environmental problems that have arisen from economic development. Although this meeting ended with few concrete results, it is an indication that people everywhere have begun to recognize that solutions to environmental problems are essential to the well-being of our planet and our own survival.

Scott E. Morris

A legend lists and explains the symbols and colors used on the map. It is called a legend because it tells the story of a map. It is important to read the map legend to find out exactly what the symbols mean because some symbols do not look like what they represent. For example, a dot stands for a town.
Every map in this atlas has a legend on it.

This legend lists and explains the colors and symbols used on the map on that page only.
The legend on the left, below, shows examples of the colors used on the maps in all the atlases in this series. Below this is a list of all symbols used on the maps in all the atlases in this series.
The legend on the right, below, is an example of a legend used in the physical atlas.

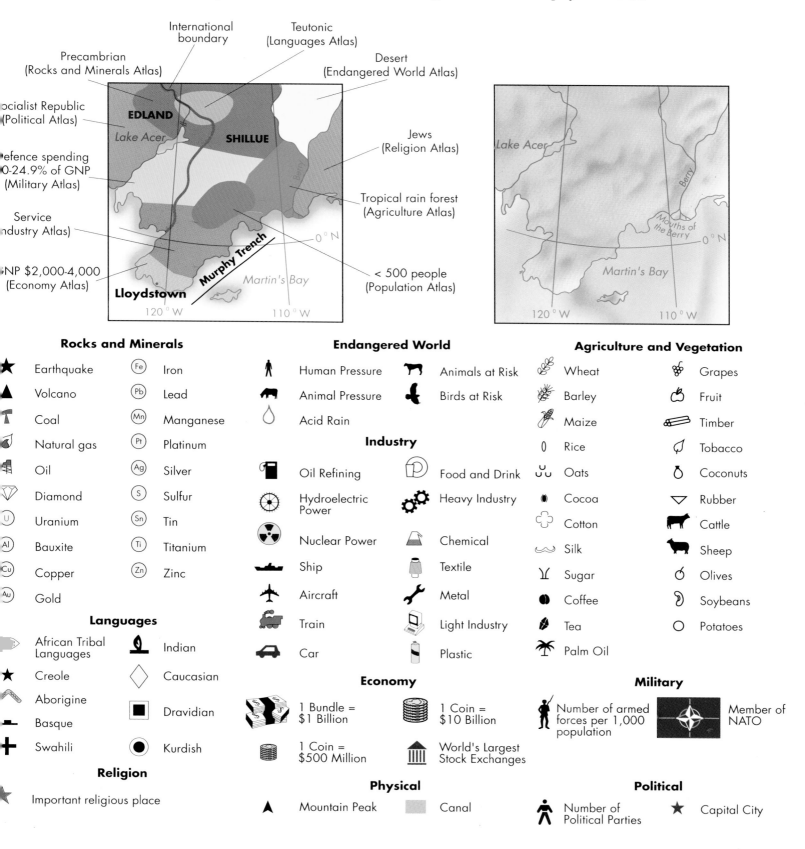

Rocks and Minerals

★ Earthquake
▲ Volcano
⚒ Coal
⛽ Natural gas
🛢 Oil
💎 Diamond
Ⓤ Uranium
Ⓐⁱ Bauxite
Ⓒᵘ Copper
Ⓐᵘ Gold

Ⓕₑ Iron
Ⓟᵇ Lead
Ⓜₙ Manganese
Ⓟₜ Platinum
Ⓐᵍ Silver
Ⓢ Sulfur
Ⓢₙ Tin
Ⓣᵢ Titanium
Ⓩₙ Zinc

Languages

African Tribal Languages
★ Creole
Aborigine
Basque
✝ Swahili

🕯 Indian
◇ Caucasian
■ Dravidian
● Kurdish

Religion

Important religious place

Endangered World

🚶 Human Pressure
🐂 Animal Pressure
💧 Acid Rain

🐄 Animals at Risk
🦅 Birds at Risk

Industry

⛽ Oil Refining
⊕ Hydroelectric Power
☢ Nuclear Power
🚢 Ship
✈ Aircraft
🚂 Train
🚗 Car

🅟 Food and Drink
⚙ Heavy Industry
⚗ Chemical
Textile
🔧 Metal
💻 Light Industry
🧴 Plastic

Economy

💵 1 Bundle = $1 Billion
🪙 1 Coin = $500 Million

🪙 1 Coin = $10 Billion
🏛 World's Largest Stock Exchanges

Physical

▲ Mountain Peak
Canal

Agriculture and Vegetation

🌾 Wheat
🌿 Barley
🌽 Maize
0 Rice
Oats
Cocoa
Cotton
Silk
Sugar
Coffee
Tea
🌴 Palm Oil

🍇 Grapes
🍎 Fruit
Timber
Tobacco
Coconuts
▽ Rubber
🐄 Cattle
🐑 Sheep
Olives
Soybeans
O Potatoes

Military

🪖 Number of armed forces per 1,000 population
✧ Member of NATO

Political

🚶 Number of Political Parties
★ Capital City

This page is a physical map of the world. It indicates where the major physical features — such as mountain ranges, plains, deserts, lakes, and rivers — are in the world. As the world is very large, the map has to be drawn at a very small scale in order to fit onto a page. This map is drawn at a scale so that 1 inch on the map, at the equator, equals 1,840 miles on the ground.

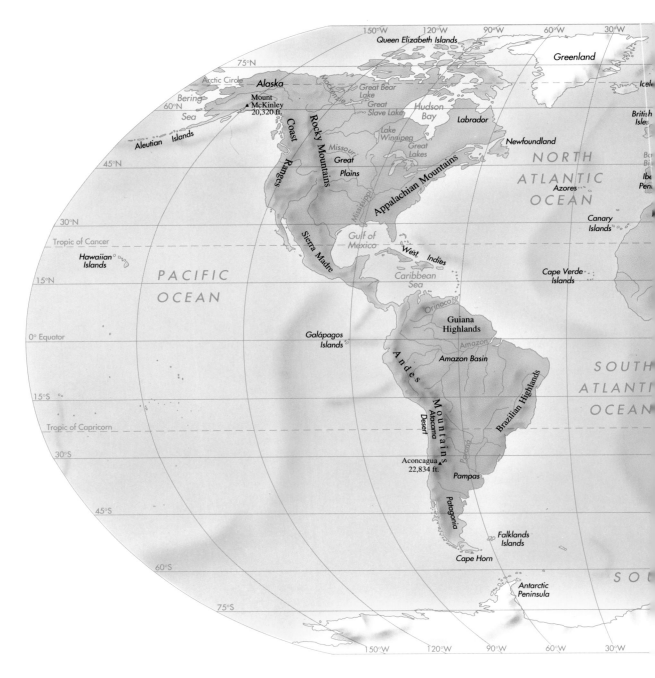

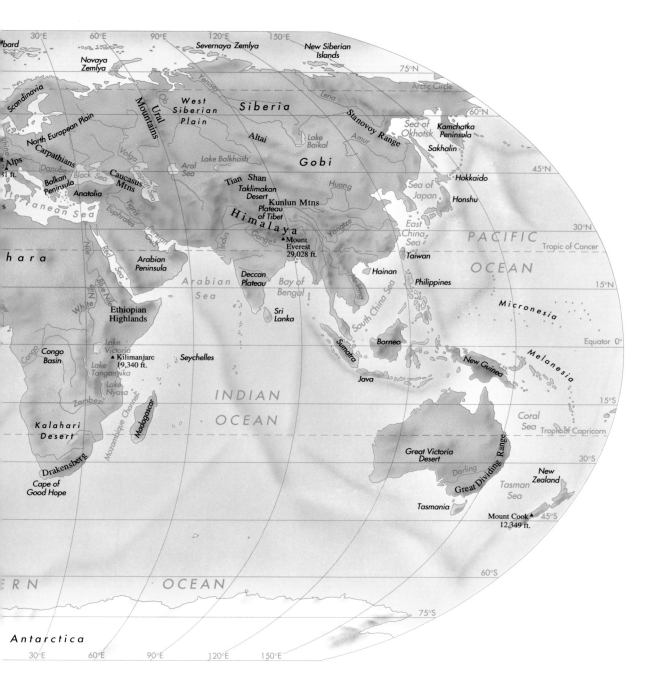

bard

30°E 60°E 90°E 120°E 150°E

Severnaya Zemlya

New Siberian
Islands

75°N

Novaya
Zemlya

Scandinavia

Ural
Mountains

West
Siberian
Plain

Siberia

Stanovoy Range

Sea of
Okhotsk

Kamchatka
Peninsula

60°N

North European Plain

Yenisey

Lena

Amur

Sakhalin

Carpathians

Altai

Lake
Baikal

Gobi

Huang

45°N

Alps

Volga

Danube

Lake Balkhash

Aral
Sea

Sea of
Japan

Hokkaido

1 ft.

Black Sea

Caucasus
Mtns

Caspian Sea

Tian Shan

Honshu

Balkan
Peninsula

Anatolia

Tigris

Taklimakan
Desert

Kunlun Mtns

Plateau
of Tibet

Himalaya

Yangtze

East
China
Sea

30°N

iterranean Sea

Euphrates

Persian Gulf

Nile

Indus

Ganges

Mount
Everest
29,028 ft.

Tropic of Cancer

PACIFIC

hara

Red Sea

Arabian
Peninsula

Arabian

Sea

Deccan
Plateau

Bay of
Bengal

Mekong

Taiwan

Hainan

OCEAN

15°N

Blue Nile

Ethiopian
Highlands

Sri
Lanka

Philippines

South China Sea

Micronesia

White Nile

Lake
Victoria

Kilimanjaro
19,340 ft.

Seychelles

Sumatra

Borneo

Equator 0°

Congo
Basin

Congo

Lake
Tanganyika

Melanesia

Lake
Nyasa

Java

New Guinea

Zambezi

INDIAN

15°S

Mozambique Channel

Madagascar

OCEAN

Coral
Sea

Kalahari
Desert

Great Victoria
Desert

Tropic of Capricorn

Great Dividing Range

Drakensberg

Darling

New
Zealand

30°S

Cape of
Good Hope

Tasman
Sea

Tasmania

Mount Cook
12,349 ft.

45°S

RN

OCEAN

60°S

75°S

Antarctica

30°E 60°E 90°E 120°E 150°E

8 World Key Map

Africa, Northern 10-11

Algeria
Benin
Burkina Faso
Cameroon
Cape Verde
Central African Republic
Chad
Djibouti
Egypt
Ethiopia
Gambia
Ghana
Guinea
Guinea-Bissau
Ivory Coast
Liberia
Libya
Mali
Mauritania
Morocco
Niger
Nigeria
Senegal
Sierra Leone
Somalia
Sudan
Togo
Tunisia
Western Sahara

Africa, Southern 12-13

Angola
Botswana
Burundi
Comoros
Congo
Equatorial Guinea
Gabon
Kenya
Lesotho
Madagascar
Malawi
Mauritius
Mozambique
Namibia
Rwanda

São Tomé & Príncipe
Seychelles
South Africa
Swaziland
Tanzania
Uganda
Zaire
Zambia
Zimbabwe

America, Central 14-15

Antigua & Barbuda
Bahamas
Barbados
Belize
Costa Rica
Cuba
Dominica

Dominican Republic
El Salvador
Grenada
Guatemala
Haiti
Honduras
Jamaica

Mexico
Nicaragua
Panama
St Kitts - Nevis
St Lucia
St Vincent
Trinidad & Tobago

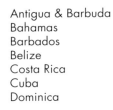

Canada 26-27

Canada

Commonwealth of Independent States 28-29

Armenia
Azerbaijan
Estonia
Georgia
Kazakhstan
Kirghizstan
Latvia
Lithuania
Moldova
Russian Federation

Tajikistan
Turkmenistan
Ukraine
Uzbekhistan

Europe 30-31

Albania
Bosnia & Herzegovina
Bulgaria
Croatia
Czechoslovakia
Finland
Greece
Hungary
Iceland
Norway

Poland
Romania
Slovenia
Sweden
Yugoslavia

Europe, Western 32-33

Andorra
Austria
Belgium
Denmark
France
Germany
Ireland
Italy
Liechtenstein
Luxembourg

Malta
Monaco
Netherlands
Portugal
San Marino
Spain
Switzerland
United Kingdom
Vatican City

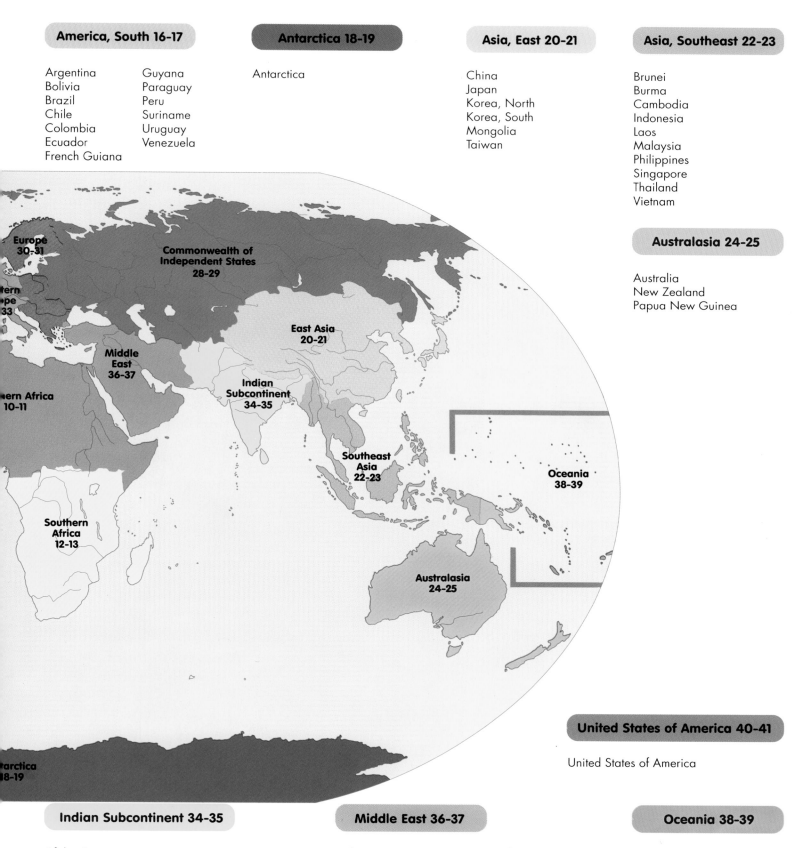

An area mostly made up of vast desert, the northern part of the African continent is home to a variety of threatened wildlife, including the Nile crocodile.

Desertification

Deserts are areas with low and unreliable rainfall and little vegetation. Semiarid areas receive more rainfall, support a little vegetation, and are often on the fringe of deserts. Semiarid areas can experience droughts during which vegetation is reduced. Humans may be forced by population growth to overgraze cattle or chop down too much wood for fuel. All these factors lead to desertification. Over one-third of the earth's surface is threatened by the process of desertification. It does not only take place on the edge of deserts. Other areas include parts of Spain, Brazil, and Argentina.

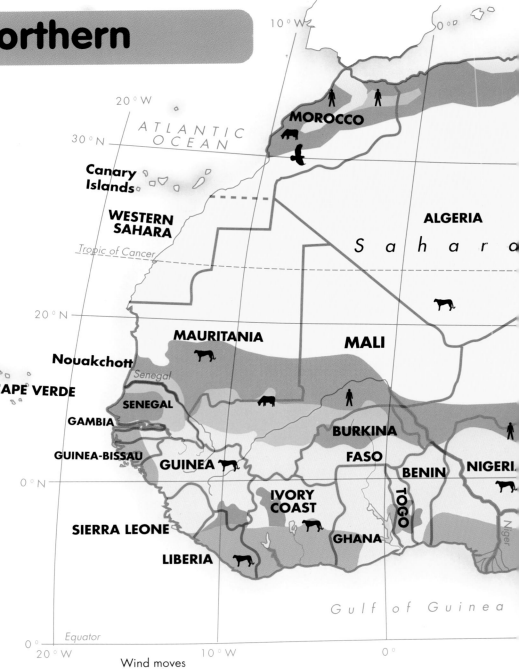

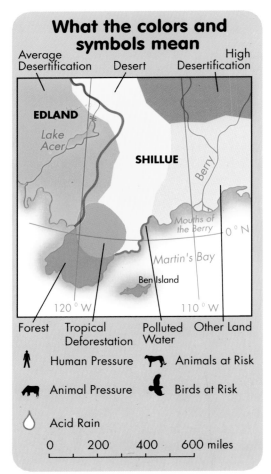

What the colors and symbols mean

- Average Desertification
- Desert
- High Desertification
- Forest
- Tropical Deforestation
- Polluted Water
- Other Land

- 🧍 Human Pressure
- 🐃 Animals at Risk
- 🐂 Animal Pressure
- 🦅 Birds at Risk
- 💧 Acid Rain

0   200   400   600 miles

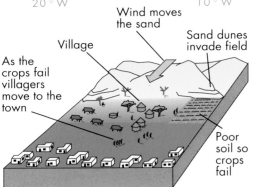

Wind moves the sand

Village

Sand dunes invade field

As the crops fail villagers move to the town

Poor soil so crops fail

Effects of desertification:

Following prolonged drought, sand dunes start to invade fields and settlements. Land without vegetation reflects solar energy and returns less moisture into the air, so rain clouds do not form. Animals collect around wells, where the remaining vegetation is overgrazed.

Nouakchott, Mauritania

In the Sahel region of Africa drought and desertification have increased soil erosion. There is littl vegetation to protect the surface from the wind. At Nouakchott ther are now more days when choking soil dust fills the air than in the late 1960s. This soil dust ends up in th Atlantic Ocean. Desertification means that crops fail and livestock die, so that people move into the city. Population for the late 1960s in Nouakchott was 20,000; it is now around 350,000. The Sahel has experienced drought for 20 years. Before the drought it was an area o savannah grassland.

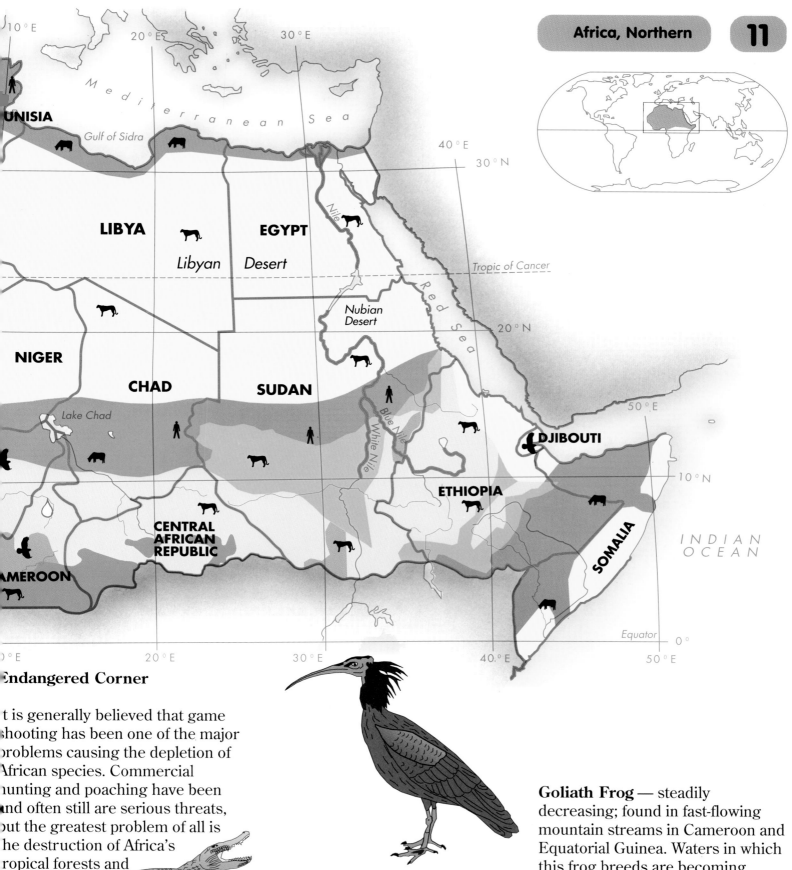

Endangered Corner

It is generally believed that game shooting has been one of the major problems causing the depletion of African species. Commercial hunting and poaching have been and often still are serious threats, but the greatest problem of all is the destruction of Africa's tropical forests and grasslands.

Nile Crocodile — numbers have been reduced due to the demand for skins. Recovery of the species following restrictions on hunting and trade has been hampered by loss of habitat.

Hermit Ibis — highly endangered; found in one small colony in Turkey and about 15 in Morocco. It used to occur in Europe and is one of the few birds to have become extinct in modern times. In Morocco the population declined from 1,000 pairs in 1930. Causes of decline include hunting and poisoning by pesticides.

Goliath Frog — steadily decreasing; found in fast-flowing mountain streams in Cameroon and Equatorial Guinea. Waters in which this frog breeds are becoming polluted. It is also used for food and collected for the live animal skin trade.

Yeheb Nut Bush — endangered bush of Ethiopia and Somalia which could be a valuable food crop for dry lands. Reduced dangerously by heavy harvesting of nuts and browsing of goats.

For years African elephants have been hunted for their ivory — a trade now banned. Most African states keep a careful control on their elephant populations but have difficulty preventing illegal poaching.

Elephant Holocaust

Despite many international campaigns to save the elephant, figures on the number of African elephants surviving slaughter by ivory poachers suggest that an elephant holocaust may be imminent.

In 1970 Africa had 2 million elephants. The population fell by 125,000 between 1987–89. If this current rate of decline continues, the African elephant will be extinct in 15 years.

International Trade in Wildlife

International trade in wildlife, worth billions of dollars every year, has been responsible for a massive decline in animal and plant species. An international treaty was drawn up in Washington in 1973, known as the Washington Convention and also as CITES (Convention on International Trade in Endangered Species of Wild Fauna and Flora.) This has created a worldwide system of controls on international trade by making permits necessary for trade. No permits are issued for trade in species that are threatened with extinction. These include: all apes, lemurs, giant pandas, many South American monkeys, great whales, cheetahs, leopards, tigers, Asian elephants, all rhinos, many birds of prey, cranes and parrots, all sea turtles, some crocodiles and lizards, giant salamanders, some mussels, orchids, and cacti.

Pygmy Hippopotamus — now rare, is found only in a small area of West Africa. The name hippopotamus means "river horse." The destruction of its forest habitat has been a major reason for its decline. Approximately 200 animals are kept in zoos.

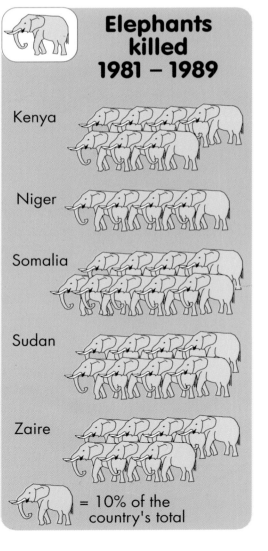

Elephants killed 1981 – 1989

Kenya

Niger

Somalia

Sudan

Zaire

= 10% of the country's total

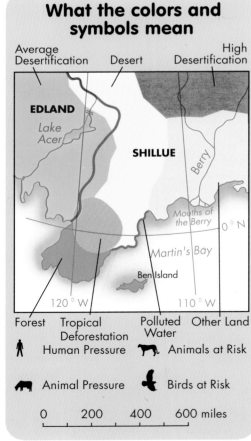

What the colors and symbols mean

Average Desertification   Desert   High Desertification

EDLAND

Lake Acer

SHILLUE

Berry

Mouths of the Berry

Martin's Bay

Ben Island

120° W   110° W

Forest   Tropical Deforestation   Polluted Water   Other Land

Human Pressure   Animals at Risk

Animal Pressure   Birds at Risk

0   200   400   600 miles

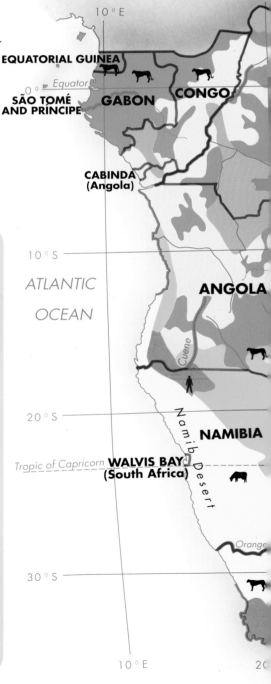

20

10° E

EQUATORIAL GUINEA

0° Equator

SÃO TOMÉ AND PRÍNCIPE   GABON   CONGO

CABINDA (Angola)

10° S

ATLANTIC OCEAN

ANGOLA

Cuene

20° S

Namib Desert

NAMIBIA

Tropic of Capricorn   WALVIS BAY (South Africa)

0° N

30° S

Orange

10° E

20

Okapi — found only in Zaire in the depths of rain forests. Because they are so shy it is hard to count them, but it is thought there are about 1,000. Their fate depends on the survival of the rain forests.

Mountain Gorilla — seriously in danger, they are found in the Virunga Volcano region in Rwanda, Uganda, and Zaire. There may be no more than 6,000 gorillas left altogether. Only 500 mountain gorillas are left, and nearly half of them live in the Virunga Volcano region.

Lemurs — in danger, they are only found in Madagascar. 80% of Madagascar's rain forests have been cleared.

How and Why We Should Conserve Species

Every man, woman, and child in the world depends on living plants and animals for their welfare. Virtually all food, nearly half the medicines we use, much of our clothing, fuel, and building materials come from living plants and animals. Our future depends on our capacity to maintain important stocks.

Humans have learned to use 3,000 plant species for food but have cultivated only 150 to the extent that they are traded widely. The great majority of people are fed by about 15 plant species.

Shrimps are certainly the world's most valuable wild animals; the total value of exports of fresh shrimps from India, Indonesia, Mexico, and other developing countries is U.S. $1 billion per year. For Panama, Pakistan, Madagascar, and some other countries, shrimps are the main source of foreign exchange.

Rattan comes from the stems of spiny climbing palms and is much used for furniture making in the tropics. Villagers use rattan for cordage, binding, thatch, medicine, and toys. It is the second most valuable forest product in Southeast Asia after timber, but there is virtually no policy for conserving it.

Map labels:
30°E, 40°E, 50°E, Equator 0°, 10°S, 20°S, Tropic of Capricorn, 30°S, 30°E, 40°E

Congo, UGANDA, KENYA, Lake Victoria, ZAIRE, RWANDA, BURUNDI, TANZANIA, Lake Tanganyika, INDIAN OCEAN, SEYCHELLES, Lake Nyasa, Ruvuma, COMOROS, MALAWI, MOZAMBIQUE, Mozambique Channel, ZAMBIA, Zambezi, ZIMBABWE, MADAGASCAR, REUNION (Fr.), TSWANA, Limpopo, Kahari Desert, Vaal, SWAZILAND, LESOTHO, SOUTH AFRICA

Paper Recycling

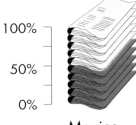

Mexico

An area of political and civil turmoil, the Central American states are also responsible for much of the region's air and sea pollution through uncontrolled emissions.

Air Pollution

Some of the worst air pollution in the world is in Mexico City. A common form of air pollution in city streets is carbon monoxide. Carbon monoxide is produced by automobile exhaust and is highly poisonous. Lead is known to be dangerous, especially to growing children. Now lead-free gasoline is available, and in several U.S. states the use of leaded gasoline is illegal.

Every year the average automobile produces nearly four times its weight in carbon dioxide. Using unleaded gasoline is a step in the right direction and opens the way to catalytic converters — which clean exhaust fumes and which only work on cars using unleaded gas. In the U.S. most cars now have catalytic converters, and they are becoming more common in Europe.

In 1989 it was reported that 2.6 billion pounds of poisons were released into the air by the U.S. Of the 320 toxicants emitted, 60 of them were cancer causing — enough to provide 10 lbs. of poison for every person in the U.S.

In 1989, 81 U.S. cities still failed to meet the required air quality standards — including the regulation of tiny bits of solid matter emitted into the air (particulate matter).

! Amazing – But True

★ Traces of lead have been found in the snows of polar ice caps. This lead comes from car exhausts in big cities thousands of miles away.

★ If all the cars in the world were parked end to end they would stretch around the equator 36 times.

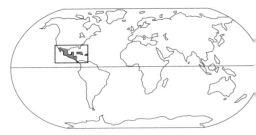

Refuse in the Ocean

Garbage in the ocean comes from land and sea. Each year ships dump million tons of plastic (including discarded fishing gear), glass, tin, wood, and biodegradable food waste into the sea. Garbage is unsightly, a health hazard, and a threat to wildlife. Ropes, nets, and plastic waste kill over 2 million seabirds and 100,000 marine mammals, plus large numbers of fish and turtles each year. In 1989 it became illegal to discard plastics from ships.

Endangered Corner

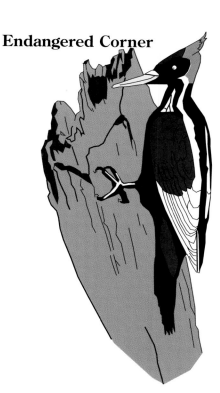

Ivory-billed Woodpecker — the second-largest and the rarest woodpecker was sighted in 1986 for the first time since 1973.
Found in the highlands of eastern Cuba, this woodpecker suffered from the clearing of the sugar plantations.

Solenodons — on the verge of extinction; found only in Cuba and Hispaniola. Deforestation and land development have eroded the habitat of this interesting little insectivore, which resembles a shrew.

Kemp's Ridley Turtle — most endangered of the sea turtles. Limited to a single nesting colony on the Rancho Nuevo beach on the Gulf of Mexico, its numbers have crashed from around 40,000 filmed in a single day in 1947 to only a few hundred today. The biggest threat now is drowning in the nets of shrimp trawlers. The rapid decline is the result of massive human exploitation of adults and eggs.

What the colors and symbols mean

Average Desertification Desert High Desertification

EDLAND
Lake Acer
SHILLUE
Berry

Mouths of the Berry

Martin's Bay

Ben Island

120°W   110°W

Forest	Tropical Deforestation	Polluted Water	Other Land

Human Pressure   Birds at Risk

Animals at Risk

0   200   400   600 miles

Map labels

ATLANTIC OCEAN

80°W   70°W   60°W   30°N

Tropic of Cancer

20°N

BAHAMAS

CUBA

DOMINICAN REPUBLIC
PUERTO RICO
Hispaniola
ANTIGUA AND BARBUDA
JAMAICA   HAITI
ST. KITTS-NEVIS
DOMINICA
ST. LUCIA
ST. VINCENT   BARBADOS
GRENADA
TRINIDAD AND TOBAGO   10°N

HONDURAS
Caribbean Sea
NICARAGUA
COSTA RICA
PANAMA

80°W   70°W   60°W

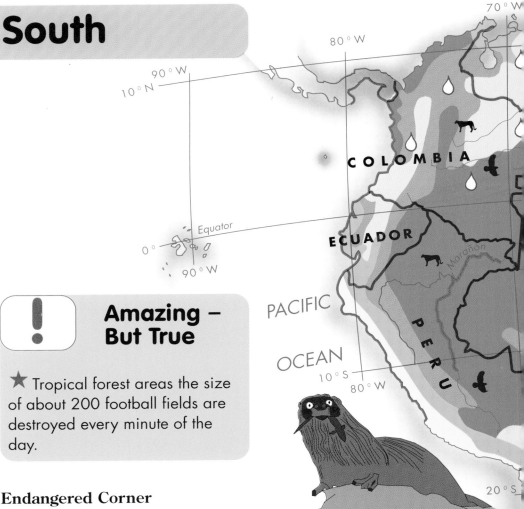

Huge areas of forest are being cleared in the region to increase available farmland. Many scientists and environmentalists fear that this could upset the delicate world balance of nature beyond recovery.

Deforestation

Twenty-five years ago tropical rain forests covered South America, Africa, and Southeast Asia. Today huge holes have been carved into the green belt. Forest land about the area of Texas was lost building the 3,000-mile-long Trans-Amazonic, a highway in Brazil. The tropical forest is the richest natural area of plants and animals. It is a hot and steamy world that is full of life — giant butterflies, bright orchids, and colorful birds. The soil is very fertile because of all the leaves that decompose, but once the trees are cut down the soil dries out and loses all its nutrients. Forests cover about one-third of the world's land cover. They protect soil, are home to plants and animals, and are a source of products for humans.

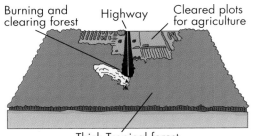

Burning and clearing forest   Highway   Cleared plots for agriculture

Thick Tropical forest

Major areas of deforestation are in the tropics, where rates of clearance have exceeded reforestation by 10 to 20 times in recent years. Tropical forests have given us a wide range of things we use in everyday life. Growing new trees in temperate areas is possible, but in the tropics, without these trees as protection the soil is quickly lost, so that once cleared, these forests may be gone forever.

Amazing – But True

★ Tropical forest areas the size of about 200 football fields are destroyed every minute of the day.

Endangered Corner

Scarlet Macaw — found in forests and wooded areas from Mexico to Brazil. With its spectacular brilliant red, blue, and green plumage and long tail, this bird is trapped and hunted in vast numbers.

Giant Otter — largest of the world's otters; found in big rivers in the Amazon Basin. It has a richly colored dark coat, which has been in great demand for the fur trade. Though legally protected now, the curious and sociable nature of this charming creature makes it easy prey for poachers.

Black Lion Tamarin — The rarest and the most endangered of the New World monkeys; by 1981 less than 100 survived. Found only in southeastern Brazil, its dramatic decline has been the result of the destruction of the forests that have been logged and cleared for plantations.

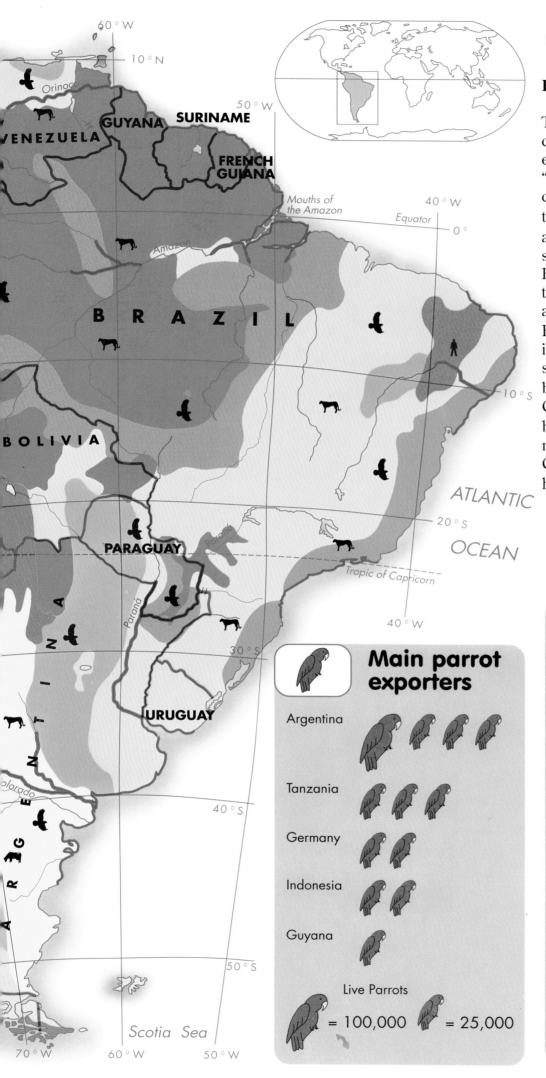

Main parrot exporters

Argentina

Tanzania

Germany

Indonesia

Guyana

Live Parrots

= 100,000   = 25,000

Effect of Deforestation

Tropical deforestation is also contributing to the greenhouse effect, caused by various "greenhouse" gases, one of which is carbon dioxide (CO_2). As trees grow, they remove CO_2 from the atmosphere by photosynthesis, storing it as carbon in their tissues. But when trees are burned or die, this carbon is returned to the atmosphere as CO_2.

Fossil fuel combustion in industrialized countries is the major source of CO_2, but many scientists believe that between 15% and 30% of CO_2 emissions come from the burning of tropical forests, mainly in the Brazilian Amazon. Currently CO_2 accounts for almost half of the greenhouse effect.

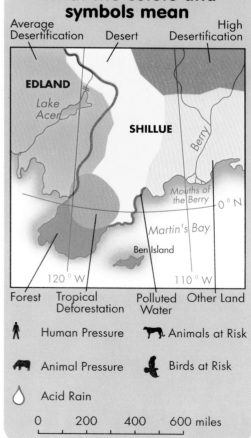

What the colors and symbols mean

Average Desertification   Desert   High Desertification

EDLAND

Lake Acer

SHILLUE

Berry

Mouths of the Berry   0° N

Martin's Bay

Ben Island

120° W   110° W

Forest   Tropical Deforestation   Polluted Water   Other Land

Human Pressure   Animals at Risk

Animal Pressure   Birds at Risk

Acid Rain

0   200   400   600 miles

Humpback Wha[l

Barely touched by man so far, Antarctica is one of the few unspoiled regions on earth. Already, however, a hole in the vital ozone layer is appearing over the continent as a result of global pollution.

Sei Whale

Ozone Layer

The ozone layer is a region in the Earth's stratosphere, between 10 to 30 miles above the surface. The ozone is a form of oxygen which protects us as it absorbs much of the harmful ultraviolet radiation that can cause skin cancer. Since 1979 scientists have noticed that the ozone layer is becoming thinner in places. The thinning is believed to be caused by a group of chemicals called chlorofluorocarbons (CFCs). These are used in aerosol spray cans, refrigerators, and polystyrene food containers. When the CFCs are released the sunlight converts them into chlorine monoxide, which in turn reacts with the ozone, removing it.

Effects of Ozone Depletion

One effect that is fairly certain is that skin cancer will increase. While a small amount of ultraviolet radiation is good for the skin, too much causes skin cancer. Ozone depletion allows too much ultraviolet radiation to reach the Earth's surface.

Endangered Corner

Krill — in the past, whales consumed vast amounts of krill, and so far little is known about the effect their reduction will have on the food chain. Several nations have begun to take catches of krill, which has a high protein value, but there are problems to overcome in making it palatable to eat and designing efficient fishing vessels.

Scotia Sea

30° W

45° W

Antarctic Circle

Weddell Sea

Filchner Ice Shelf

Drake Passage

60° W

75° W

50° S

55° S

Bellingshausen Sea

90° W

60° S

65° S

70° S

75° S

80° S

85° S

105° W

SOUTHERN OCEAN

Ross Sea

120° W

135° W

165° W

150° W

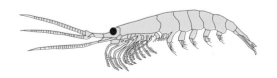

The Blue Whale — weighs as much as 30 elephants or 1,600 people (up to 66,000 lbs. on average). It is as long as three railroad cars, yet in the water it is sleek and graceful.

Although Antarctica supports very little life, the Antarctic seas are highly fertile and biologically productive, supporting an abundance of birds, seals, whales, fish, and squid, all directly or indirectly dependent on krill. This remarkable environment is one of the ecosystems least affected by human activities, but even here the influence of humans is apparent. The main influence is the decimation of the elephant seals, fur seals, and great whales.

Whaling

Commercial whalers have exploited almost every whale species, forcing many populations to the brink of extinction. With current controls on whale hunting, international trade in whale products has diminished from its once staggering volume. Whale meat and oil are the major whale commodities still in trade today, yet both natural and synthetic substitutes for both are available.

The limits on whaling do not seem to have increased the stock of whales. However they are still threatened.

Sperm Whale

Whales

The blue, humpback, fin, sei, and sperm whales have been hunted one after the other until numbers of each were too low to make whaling viable. Blue whales, the largest creatures ever to live on earth, are now down to less than 1% of their original population, and numbers are not increasing even after years of protection.

Fin Whale

Ozone "hole" in 1987

Ozone "hole" in 1981

South Pole

Mackenzie Bay

Davis Sea

SOUTHERN OCEAN

The Ozone "Hole"

The ozone layer over Antarctica thins every year during the spring, and at this time of the year the "hole" in the ozone is largest. A hole first appeared in 1981, and it has been growing every year. By 1986 it was the size of the U.S. Look at the map to see the change in the ozone "hole" from 1981 to 1987. In 1990 the United States and 55 other nations agreed to end the production of CFCs by the year 2000 in the hope that this will stop the ozone "hole" from increasing in size.

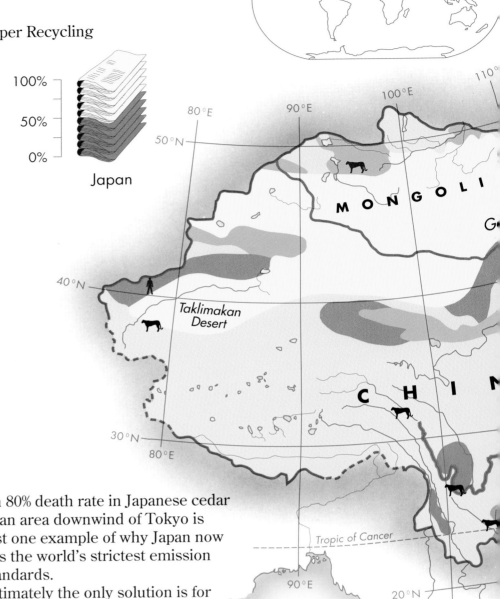

Hunted for sport over centuries and its natural habitat now threatened by the spread of human civilization, the Asian tiger is perhaps the foremost symbol of endangered species in the region.

Acid Rain

Fossil fuels when burned produce sulfur and nitrogen, which react with damp air to make sulfuric and nitric acid. If the air is dry the reaction takes place very slowly. This has created an international problem since fumes from factory chimneys in Britain may fall as acid rain over Scandinavia. There lakes and river have become acidic, damaging plant life and killing fish. Also soil has been affected, and so forests are dying. A similar problem exists in North America, where fumes from factories in the U.S. are blown northward to Canada. As a result, the famous Canadian maple trees are dying.

The damage is caused not only by rain that is more acidic than it should be but by snow, fog, and dry dust that contain sulfur and nitrogen oxides. It is estimated that the burning of fossil fuels has doubled the amount of sulfur dioxide over the surface of the earth. In the polluted industrial areas there has been a ninefold increase.

How Acid Rain is formed

Sulfur dioxide and nitrogen oxide mix with water droplets.

This then falls as sulfuric acid and nitric acid rain - acid rain and acid snow.

Melting acid snow

Paper Recycling

100%
50%
0%

Japan

An 80% death rate in Japanese cedar in an area downwind of Tokyo is just one example of why Japan now has the world's strictest emission standards.
Ultimately the only solution is for all nations to reduce consumption of fossil fuels by using energy more effectively, by increasing recycling of paper and metals, and by generating more power from alternative energy sources.

Taklimakan Desert

MONGOLIA

G

CHINA

Tropic of Cancer

Endangered Corner

Tiger — until recently there were eight different varieties of tiger in different parts of Asia. One of them is extinct — the Bali Tiger. In the past 50 years the number of tigers has gone from 100,000 to 5,000, mainly due to the destruction of the forests. Despite legal protection in all countries, the tiger is still hunted.

★ The Japanese throw away 16 million pairs of chopsticks every day. These are all made from wood harvested in tropical rain forests.

★ One person uses enough items of wood a year to equal a tree 100 feet tall.

Toxic Waste

Toxic materials disposed of in the sea can cause serious problems as they accumulate in the food chain. In Minamata Bay, Japan, between 1952 and 1960, over 2,000 people suffered from crippling mental disorders and physical deformities, and over 40 died from eating shellfish which had accumulated methyl mercury.

Giant Panda — affected by the bamboo forests being cut down to make farming land, it is now found only in the dense area of bamboo forests of Western China. Pandas spend as many as twelve hours a day feeding. Today it is estimated that about 1,000 of these "bei-shung" remain. They now receive protection from the Chinese Government.

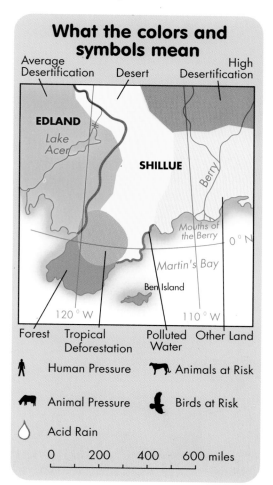

What the colors and symbols mean

Average Desertification   Desert   High Desertification

EDLAND

Lake Acer

SHILLUE

Berry

Mouths of the Berry   0° N

Martin's Bay

Ben Island

120° W   110° W

Forest	Tropical Deforestation	Polluted Water	Other Land

🚶 Human Pressure   🐃 Animals at Risk

🐂 Animal Pressure   🐾 Birds at Risk

💧 Acid Rain

0   200   400   600 miles

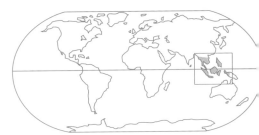

Southeast Asia is the base of an internationally outlawed ivory trade, threatening the existence of both African and Asian elephant populations — animals already endangered by the loss of their natural habitat to human exploitation.

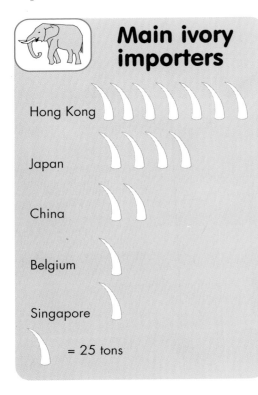

Main ivory importers

Hong Kong

Japan

China

Belgium

Singapore

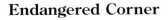
= 25 tons

Ocean Pollution

Many of the world's cities support a large population and heavy industry. Vast quantities of industrial waste are either dumped into the sea or into rivers that drain to the ocean. Human waste is organic and can be recycled by the sea, but much industrial waste is inorganic and does not break down so easily. Over 100,000 different chemicals find their way into the sea. 85% of the 20 billion tons of pollution put into the oceans annually comes from the land. 90% of that pollution stays in the coastal area, causing serious environmental and health problems. In Southeast Asia approximately one quarter of the people living at or near the coast make their living from the sea. These waters are also some of the most heavily polluted by sewage. Shellfish like oysters and mussels are among the first to be seriously affected.

Endangered Corner

Rafflesia — this plant, found in Indonesia, has the largest flower in the world. It is under threat partly from destruction and disturbance of the rain forests and partly from the attention it attracts. It is being collected for medicine and for novelty and many botanists have been unable to resist acquiring it.

Orangutan — one of the largest and most appealing of the apes, the orangutan lives in the large islands of Sumatra and Borneo. Arboreal, slow-moving, solitary, and independent, there are few animals that pose less threat to humans. Human activity, however, threatens to deprive this creature of its forest habitat.

Bumblebee Bat — only discovered by scientists in 1974, this tiny bat from Thailand weighs only 0.07 ounces. It is threatened by proposed hydroelectric projects that would flood its cave habitat.

BURMA

LAOS

THAILAND

Mekong

VIETNAM

CAMBODIA

Andaman Sea

Gulf of Thailand

Tropic of Cancer

30°N

20°N

10°N

0°

10°S

100°E

110

M A L

Kuala Lumpur

SINGAPORE

Equator

Sumatra

Ja

100°E

110

Main ivory exporters

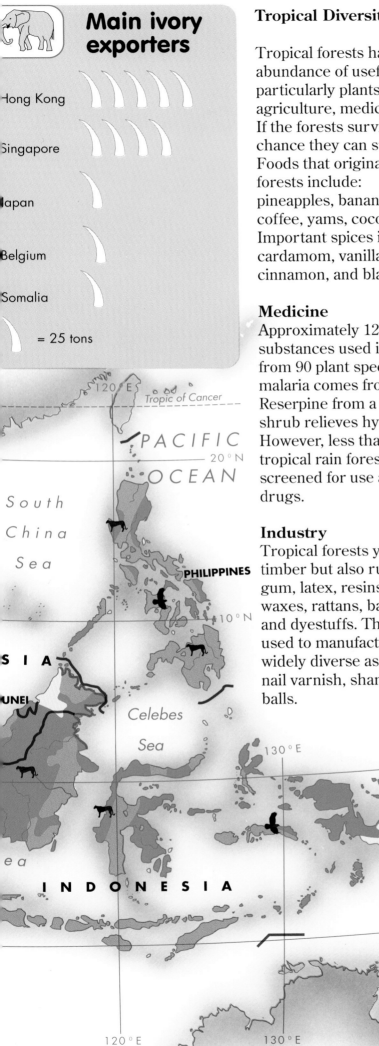

Hong Kong

Singapore

Japan

Belgium

Somalia

= 25 tons

Tropical Diversity

Tropical forests have supplied an abundance of useful species — particularly plants for food and agriculture, medicine and industry. If the forests survive there is a good chance they can supply many more. Foods that originated from tropical forests include:
pineapples, bananas, citrus fruits, coffee, yams, cocoa, and sago. Important spices include:
cardamom, vanilla, nutmeg, cinnamon, and black pepper.

Medicine
Approximately 120 pure chemical substances used in medicine come from 90 plant species. Quinine for malaria comes from a tree in Peru. Reserpine from a Southeast Asian shrub relieves hypertension. However, less than 1% of known tropical rain forest plants have been screened for use as life-saving drugs.

Industry
Tropical forests yield not only timber but also rubber, edible oils, gum, latex, resins, tannins, steroids, waxes, rattans, bamboo, flavorings, and dyestuffs. These materials are used to manufacture goods as widely diverse as chewing gum and nail varnish, shampoo and golf balls.

Main primate exporters

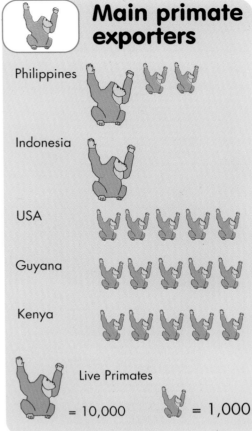

Philippines

Indonesia

USA

Guyana

Kenya

Live Primates

= 10,000   = 1,000

What the colors and symbols mean

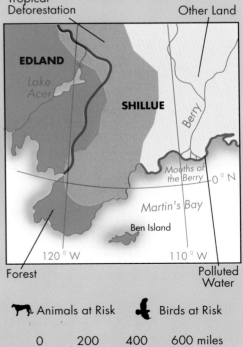

Tropical Deforestation

Other Land

EDLAND

Lake Acer

SHILLUE

Berry

Mouths of the Berry

Martin's Bay

Ben Island

Forest

Polluted Water

120° W   110° W

Animals at Risk   Birds at Risk

0   200   400   600 miles

Dominated by the huge continent of Australia, the land area is largely made up of desert, fringed by lightly populated temperate areas.

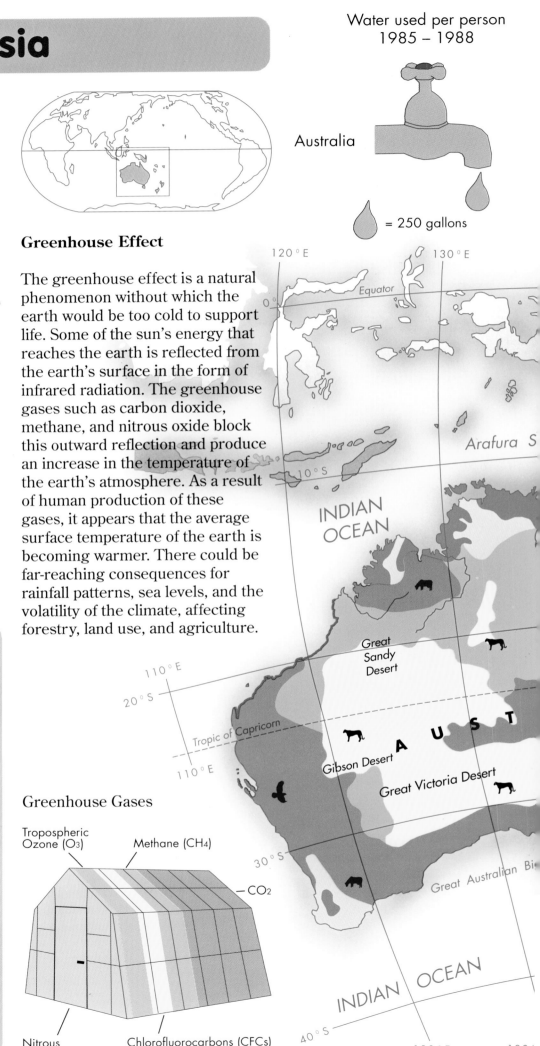

Water used per person 1985 – 1988

Australia

= 250 gallons

Endangered Corner

Queen Alexandra's Birdwing Butterfly — the world's largest butterfly is also the most threatened. The beauty of its 10-inch wingspan as it soars across the jungles of Papua New Guinea may soon be no more than a memory. It has been protected by strictly enforced laws since 1966.

Greenhouse Effect

The greenhouse effect is a natural phenomenon without which the earth would be too cold to support life. Some of the sun's energy that reaches the earth is reflected from the earth's surface in the form of infrared radiation. The greenhouse gases such as carbon dioxide, methane, and nitrous oxide block this outward reflection and produce an increase in the temperature of the earth's atmosphere. As a result of human production of these gases, it appears that the average surface temperature of the earth is becoming warmer. There could be far-reaching consequences for rainfall patterns, sea levels, and the volatility of the climate, affecting forestry, land use, and agriculture.

What the colors and symbols mean

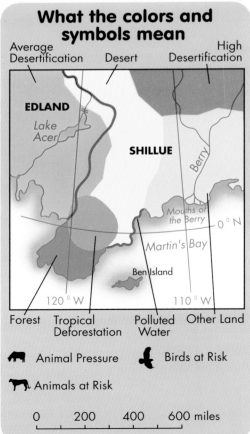

Average Desertification Desert High Desertification

EDLAND
Lake Acer
SHILLUE
Berry
Mouths of the Berry
0° N
Martin's Bay
Ben Island
120° W   110° W

Forest   Tropical Deforestation   Polluted Water   Other Land

🐃 Animal Pressure   🦅 Birds at Risk

🐂 Animals at Risk

```
0    200    400    600 miles
```

Greenhouse Gases

Tropospheric Ozone (O_3)   Methane (CH_4)

— CO_2

Nitrous Oxide (N_2O)   Chlorofluorocarbons (CFCs) and Halons

120° E   130° E

Equator

Arafura S

10° S

INDIAN OCEAN

Great Sandy Desert

110° E

20° S

Tropic of Capricorn

110° E

Gibson Desert   A U S T

Great Victoria Desert

30° S

Great Australian Bi

INDIAN OCEAN

40° S

120° E   130°

Amazing – But True

★ In Britain glass bottles are sorted by color, then melted down and reused.

★ Scientists estimate that one wild species becomes extinct every hour.

Biological Control

Some species are particularly important because they control other species whose populations would otherwise have grown to pest proportions. An early example of this was the domestication of the cat in ancient Egypt to keep down rats and mice that were ravaging corn stores. Indian scientists have recently supplied parasites to Papua New Guinea to control stem-boring caterpillars. The United States has managed to control 120 insect pests by importing 223 of their natural enemies. However, there are still dangers from experimenting with ecology without real knowledge of all the implications. In Hawaii no fewer than 17 insects and mollusks have been introduced to control the giant African snail, itself misguidedly introduced in 1936 and now a crop pest. Now the native Hawaiian snails are threatened with extinction.

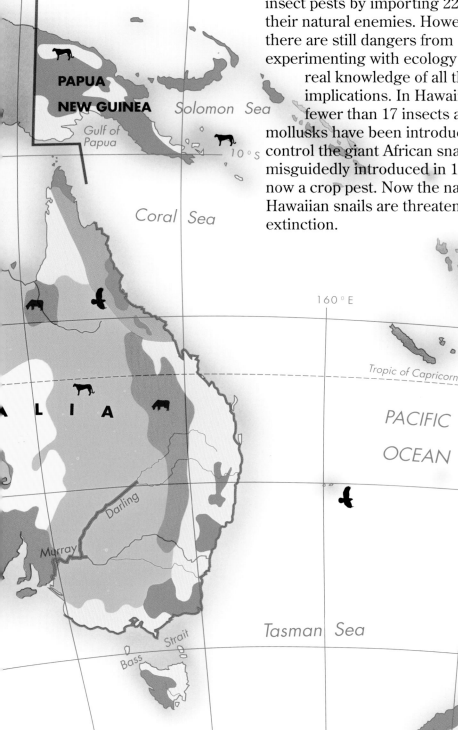

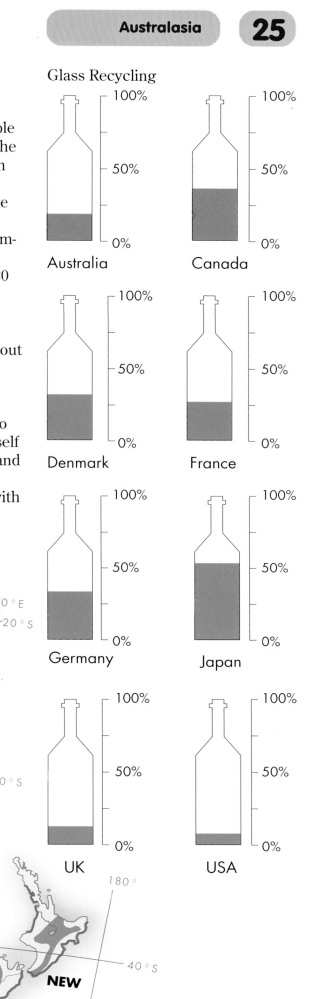

Glass Recycling

Australia

Canada

Denmark

France

Germany

Japan

UK

USA

Although the human population of the country is small compared to its vast size, much can be done to control the hunting and trapping of endangered species. The polar bear is now at risk.

Dos and Don'ts for Wildlife Preservation

- Don't leave litter. It is unsightly and small animals like mice or lizards can suffocate in old bottles or cans.

- Don't pick flowers until you know if you may. Some plants are protected by law.

- Don't disturb birds' nests or their eggs. Don't take young animals from where you find them. They can look after themselves.

- Do enjoy the countryside. Walk and enjoy it but leave it as you found it.

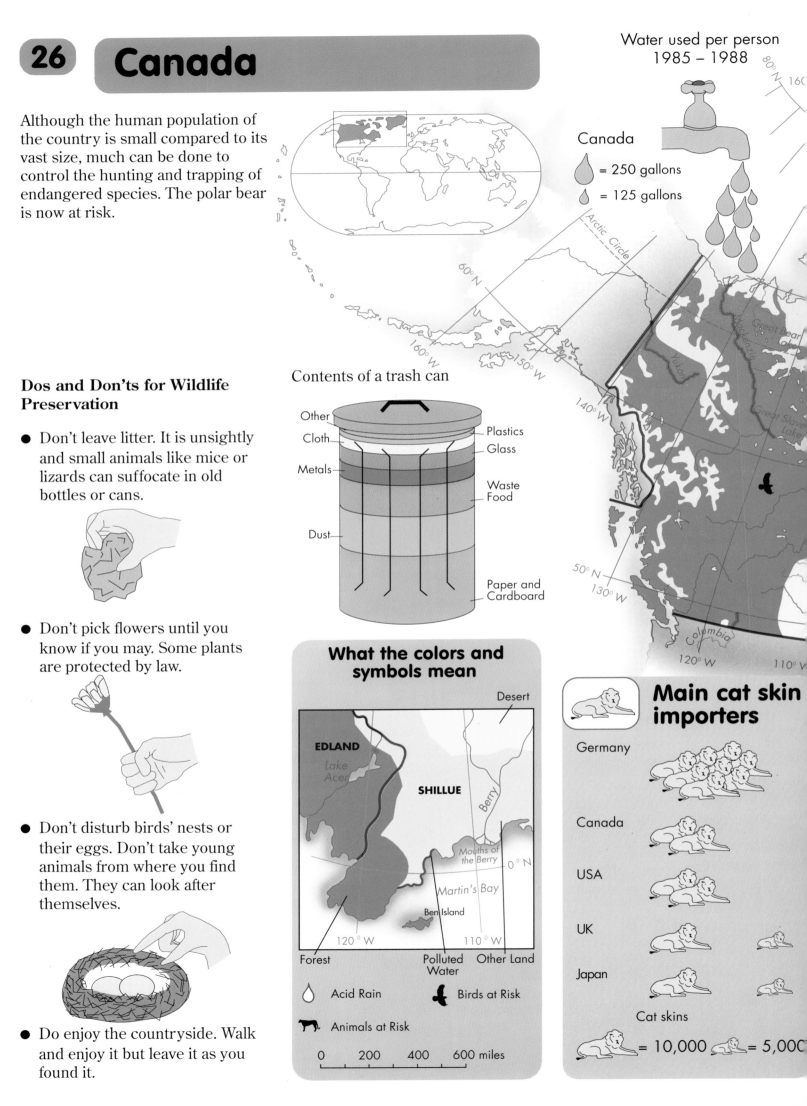

Water used per person 1985 – 1988

Canada

= 250 gallons

= 125 gallons

Contents of a trash can

Other
Cloth
Metals
Dust
Plastics
Glass
Waste Food
Paper and Cardboard

What the colors and symbols mean

EDLAND
Lake Acer
SHILLUE
Berry
Desert
Mouths of the Berry
Martin's Bay
Ben Island
0° N
120° W   110° W

Forest
Polluted Water
Other Land

Acid Rain   Birds at Risk

Animals at Risk

0   200   400   600 miles

Main cat skin importers

Germany

Canada

USA

UK

Japan

Cat skins

= 10,000   = 5,000

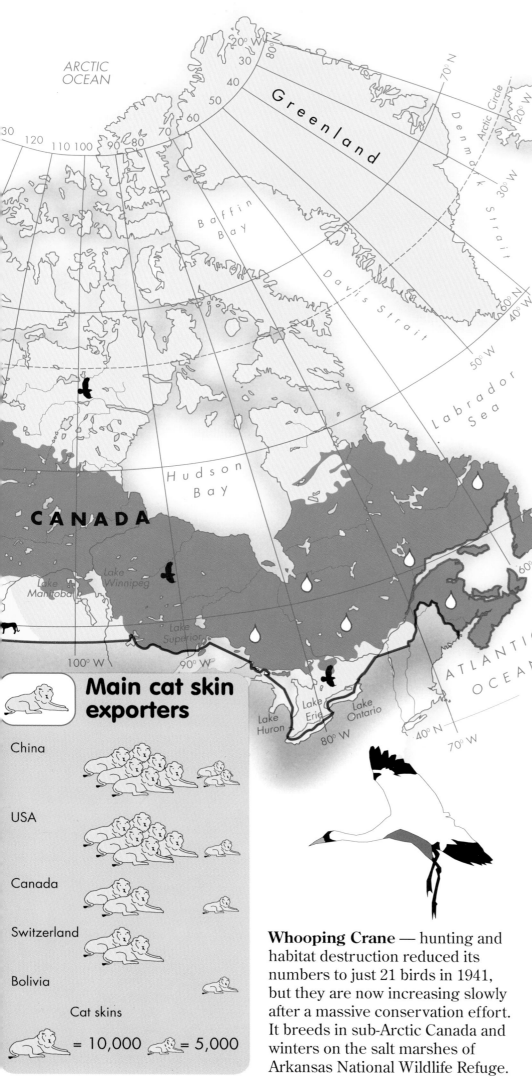

Recycling

Recycling involves the reprocessing of waste into new items:
Paper can be pulped again and made into new paper goods, broken glass can be melted down.
Kitchen refuse and organic matter can be used to make compost, bones can be made into glue.
Paints and high-grade carbon for sugar refining and cloth can be converted to upholstery and blankets.

If we recycled, pollution would be cut down. The reuse of scrap iron by steel mills leads to a reduction in air and water pollution.

Paper Recycling

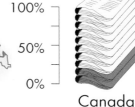

100%

50%

0%

Canada

Endangered Corner

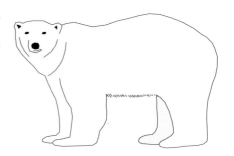

Polar Bear — this magnificent ice bear lives in the snowy habitat of the Arctic. Once a threatened species; with a recent conservation agreement between the five countries that have bear populations — Denmark (Greenland), Canada, Norway, CIS, and USA — the outlook for the bear is improving, and its population is stable.
The polar bear eats seals and small mammals, birds, and eggs.
In Canada, local peoples like Inuit and other Indians are allowed to kill a small number under license.

Main cat skin exporters

China

USA

Canada

Switzerland

Bolivia

Cat skins

= 10,000   = 5,000

Whooping Crane — hunting and habitat destruction reduced its numbers to just 21 birds in 1941, but they are now increasing slowly after a massive conservation effort. It breeds in sub-Arctic Canada and winters on the salt marshes of Arkansas National Wildlife Refuge.

The danger of inadequate protection of the environment was shown horribly at Chernobyl in 1984, and the risk of further radioactive contamination remains in a region beset with political and economic problems.

Overfishing

The oceans of the world provide over 80 million tons of fish a year. Fish are an important food in many countries, and over a third of the fish caught are fed to animals or used as fertilizers.

Fish are not farmed but hunted. Fishermen have to find areas rich in fish and catch them. The oceans have plenty of fish as long as the resource is not exploited. Many countries set up 200-mile fishing zones around their coasts so that they can control fishing; however beyond those areas the deep-sea fleets of richer nations such as Japan and the former Soviet Union are emptying the seas of fish.

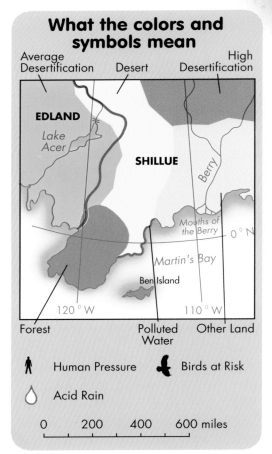

What the colors and symbols mean

Average Desertification   Desert   High Desertification

EDLAND

Lake Acer

SHILLUE

Berry

Mouths of the Berry   0° N

Martin's Bay

Ben Island

120° W   110° W

Forest   Polluted Water   Other Land

Human Pressure   Birds at Risk

Acid Rain

0   200   400   600 miles

Radioactive Waste

A radioactive atom disintegrates by emitting particles — radioactive decay. It can be slow, taking as long as thousands of years. The particles emitted may be alpha, beta, or gamma, and each has different biological and physical effects. Nuclear plants discharge radioactive waste into the air, rivers, and sea. But the most serious and widespread radioactive pollution is caused by accidents such as those at Three Mile Island in the U.S. and Chernobyl in the former Soviet Union. High doses of radioactivity quickly kill animals; lower doses cause cancers, tumors, leukemia, and premature death. Very low doses may cause mutations that result in genetic abnormalities.

80°E 100°E 120°E

180°

ARCTIC OCEAN

East Siberian Sea

70°N

Arctic Circle

60°N

180°

Bering Sea

50°N

Lena

Lena

Sea of Okhotsk

160°E

PACIFIC OCEAN

OF INDEPENDENT STATES

Amur

120°E

40°N

100°E

140°E

40°N

Endangered Corner

Lynx — still killed for the fur trade or as a pest, there is concern for this solidly built cat with ear tufts. Its furred feet act as snowshoes during the winter in the northern regions where it is found.

Radioactive materials accumulate in marine life and can pass up the food chain, or they can reach humans by contaminated sea spray and in sediments moving shoreward. The sea was once considered the perfect disposal site for drums of radioactive waste. This practice has now been stopped, but there is still concern about how long the waste containers will survive in the ocean depths. They may well be a time bomb.

Siberian Crane — a rare and extremely beautiful white crane that breeds on the tundras of the CIS in two separate groups. Some of the western flock, numbering about 60 birds, winter in Iran, while the rest winter in India. The eastern flock migrate to the marshes of southern China. The most recent count of this flock (1985) was 1,350 birds. In their wintering grounds, the birds feed only on submerged sedge tubers, so they are dependent on large, shallow wetlands for their survival.

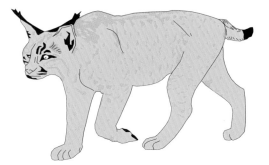

Intensely farmed and industrialized, Europe is acutely aware of the threat its own population poses to the environment. All nations are now imposing controls to limit the extent of harmful developments.

Municipal Waste

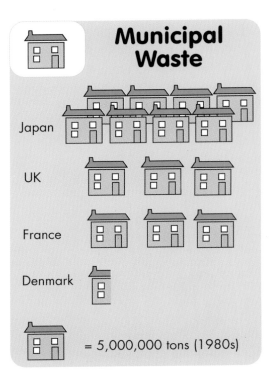

Japan

UK

France

Denmark

= 5,000,000 tons (1980s)

Hazardous Waste

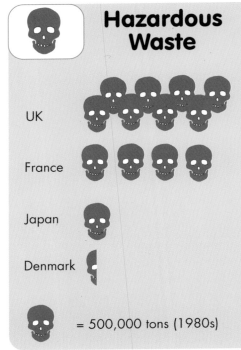

UK

France

Japan

Denmark

= 500,000 tons (1980s)

Endangered Corner

Wolf — although the wolf is still quite common in Alaska, North America, and parts of the former Soviet Union, it is becoming rare and endangered in Europe. Wolves live in a wide range of habitats from tundra to forest and open plains, and they prey on large wild animals such as deer. Where these animals have become rare, wolves have preyed on domestic stock and come into conflict with farmers.

White-tailed Sea Eagle — there are less than 750 pairs of this magnificent bird, and about half are found in Norway. It is now being reintroduced into the Isle of Rhum on the west coast of Scotland.

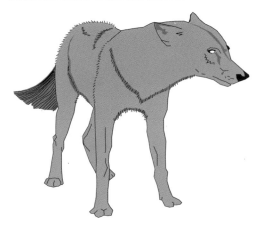

Forests Lost
Finland

Sweden

! **Amazing – But True**

★ Great Britain uses 2 trees' worth of paper per person each year and throws away no less than 4 billion aluminum drink cans each year.

★ Over half of the aluminum drink cans in the U.S. are melted down and reused.

Agricultural Waste

Nutrients from fertilizers cause oxygen depletion and plankton blooms. DDT reduces photosynthesis by phytoplankton with subsequent effects for the whole marine food web. Insecticides threaten wildlife at the top of the food chain like the peregrine falcon, which suffers thinning of its eggs. Fish can accumulate poisons. High levels of tributyltin (TBT) an antifoulant used to paint boats, have been discovered in salmon.

Marine food web

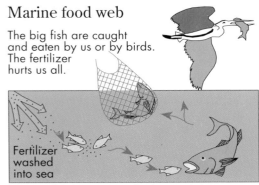

The big fish are caught and eaten by us or by birds. The fertilizer hurts us all.

Fertilizer washed into sea

The small fish are eaten by bigger fish.

Soil Erosion

This natural process is the movement of soil off the land by water, wind, ice, or landslides. The soil is carried away and deposited in a different part of the land or in the sea. Where humans affect the natural vegetation cover the erosion rates are increased. If this is greater than the production of new soil, it is a serious problem.

The United States is one of the few countries that have analyzed their soil loss in detail: one estimate put the loss at 5 billion tons a year. To maintain crop yields in the face of eroding soil, farmers spend more on chemicals and fertilizers. These are washed into the waterways, pollute the water, and damage fish life. Soil erosion causes a decline in fish populations, and the destruction of coral reefs, and decreases the amount of water stored in reservoirs.

What the colors and symbols mean

Forest   Other Land   High Desertification

EDLAND

Lake Acer

SHILLUE

Berry

Mouths of the Berry   0° N

Martin's Bay

Ben Island

120° W   110° W

Average Desertification   Polluted Water

🧍 Human Pressure   🐂 Animals at Risk

💧 Acid Rain   🦅 Birds at Risk

0   200   400   600 miles

? **Did You Know**

★ Germany's annual acid rain bill is around $2 billion a year. This is the amount of money needed to repair damage caused by air pollution to forests and buildings.

★ One of the most polluted bodies of water on Earth is the Mediterranean Sea.

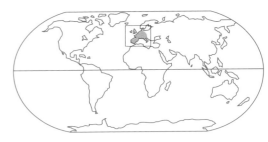

Home to some of the world's most intensive industry and a wealthy consumer society, Western Europe has seen serious pollution affect its seas, rivers, and forests.

Forests Lost

UK

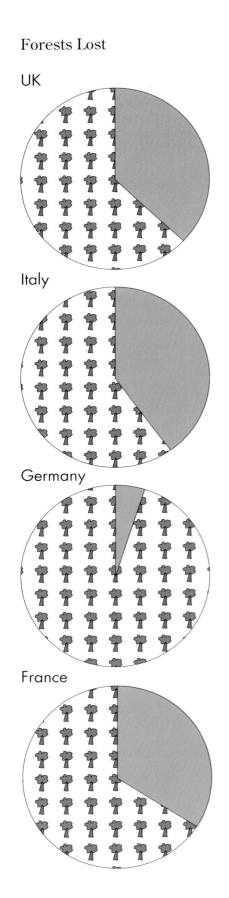

Italy

Germany

France

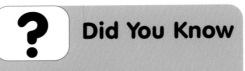

? Did You Know

★ More than one-third of the Black Forest in Germany is dying. This is thought to be due to the exhausts from buses, cars, and trucks.

Land Pollution

There has been an increasing need for more food since the 1940s, when a tremendous growth in the world's population started. The response has been to increase the area of land used to grow food. Agriculture has also become more intensive so that more crops can be harvested from the land under cultivation. This intensive agriculture means using more and better machinery, expanding the areas under irrigation, and increasing the use of chemical fertilizers and pesticides. Fertilizers pollute the water when they are washed out of the soil. Pollution of drinking water, especially by nitrate fertilizers, is becoming a serious problem in areas of intensive agriculture.

Farmers in Western Europe have been encouraged by governments to produce more food. This has resulted in "overproduction" of some foods. This unwanted food is stored as "mountains." The European Community's butter mountain reached a peak of 1.5 million tons in 1986. This cost $1 million a day to store. Now the European Community is trying to reduce this overproduction, and farmers in many parts of Western Europe are returning fields to their natural conditions to try to rectify the impact of modern agriculture on the environment.

Paper Recycling

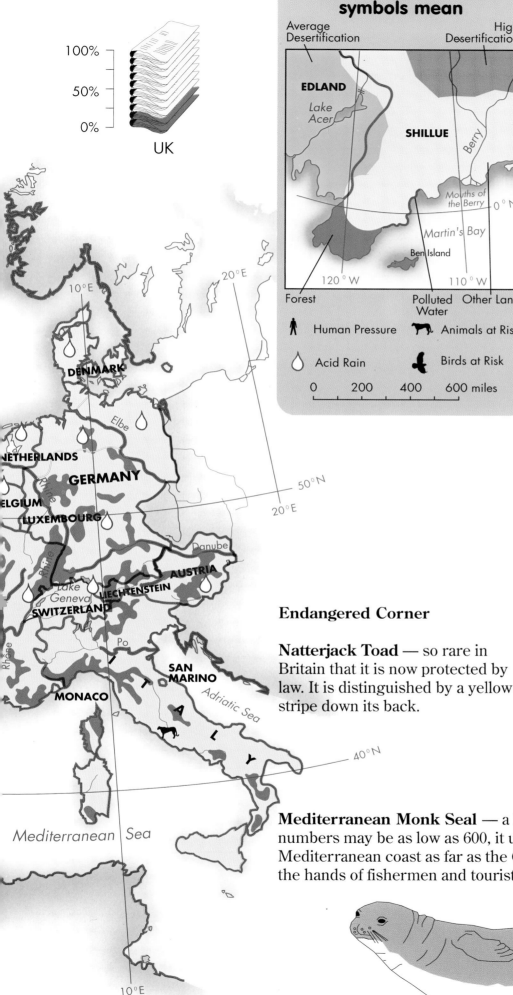

100%

50%

0%

UK

What the colors and symbols mean

Average Desertification

High Desertification

EDLAND

Lake Acer

SHILLUE

Berry

Mouths of the Berry

0° N

Martin's Bay

Ben Island

120° W

110° W

Forest

Polluted Water

Other Land

👤 Human Pressure

🐕 Animals at Risk

💧 Acid Rain

🦅 Birds at Risk

0   200   400   600 miles

Sewage Pollution

Sewage is unsightly and contains bacteria that can cause diseases such as polio, hepatitis, and ear infections. It can produce plankton or algal blooms that reduce the oxygen bacteria need to break down sewage. Certain plankton species are toxic to fish and mammals and cause paralytic shellfish poisoning. Sewage contains toxic substances because heavy industrial plants are sometimes connected to domestic sewers. Sewage treatment results in sludge, which is frequently dumped at sea.

Effects of Pollution

The seashore and beach are places where people enjoy themselves on vacation. In Britain 40% of the beaches fall below the recommended health standards laid down by the European Community. The main problem is human sewage, but on many beaches vacationers are forced to pick their way through sticky black oil, broken glass, and other debris. The water pollution is causing a sticky brown foam to appear on the sea.

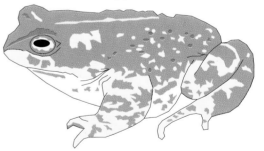

Endangered Corner

Natterjack Toad — so rare in Britain that it is now protected by law. It is distinguished by a yellow stripe down its back.

Mediterranean Monk Seal — a highly endangered species whose numbers may be as low as 600, it used to be found all along the Mediterranean coast as far as the Canary Islands. It has suffered greatly at the hands of fishermen and tourists.

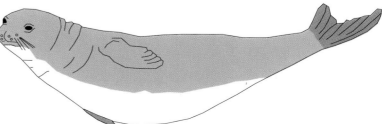

Heavily populated and recently industrialized, the countries of the area have yet to adjust their march of progress to meet the needs of their environment. Water shortages and inadequate waste control are major problems.

Water Shortages

In the industrial nations it is usually taken for granted that the water is fit for drinking. Contaminated water is one of the biggest dangers for children in the developing world.

The average family of four uses 770 gallons of water every week. One-third is used for flushing toilets, more than any other use in the home.

Domestic Water Used

One washing mashine load uses 22 gallons of water.

One dishwasher load uses 11 gallons of water.

One toilet flush uses 2 gallons of water.

One bath uses 18 gallons of water.

AFGHANISTAN

PAKISTAN

Jhelum

Chenab

Ravi

Indus

Jumna

Tropic of Cancer

Gulf of Kutch

Narbada

I N D

20°N

Arabian Sea

Krishna

Krishna

Godavari

10°N

Cauvery

70°E

Gulf of Mannar

SRI LANKA

MALDIVES

80°E

I N D I A N

Indian Python — this large and beautiful snake is declining in population and has become extinct in places due to the heavy export of python skins. Trade in python skins is now strictly regulated.

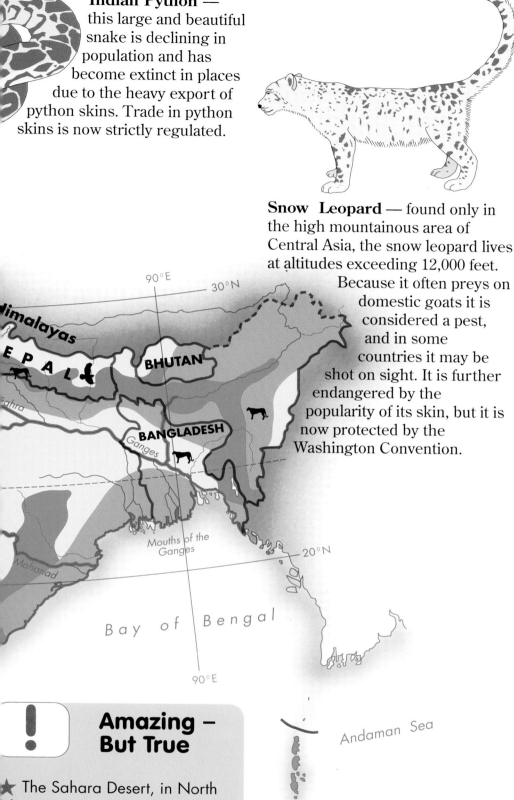

Snow Leopard — found only in the high mountainous area of Central Asia, the snow leopard lives at altitudes exceeding 12,000 feet. Because it often preys on domestic goats it is considered a pest, and in some countries it may be shot on sight. It is further endangered by the popularity of its skin, but it is now protected by the Washington Convention.

Water Erosion

Water erosion is worst where the rainfall is high and vegetation is removed. This is most noticeable on the slopes of hills and mountains where the force of the water flowing can sweep masses of fertile topsoil into streams and rivers and eventually to the sea. Much of the fertile silt being reclaimed in the Ganges Delta in Bangladesh came from the sides of Himalayan slopes 1,000 miles away in Nepal. The United States has lost one-third of its topsoil across the nation since farming began.

Unless there are dramatic changes in farming policies both in the developed and developing worlds, a further 355,000 million tons of soil will be eroded and up to 1 million square miles of desert formed by the year 2000.

Amazing – But True

★ The Sahara Desert, in North Africa, is expanding southward at an average rate of 5 miles a year.

★ Approximately half the world's population uses wood for cooking and heating.

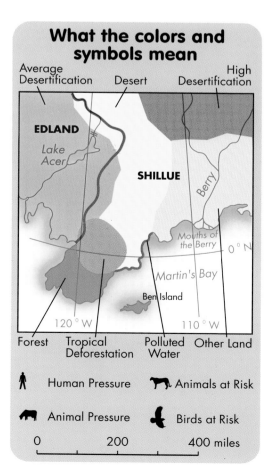

What the colors and symbols mean

Average Desertification	Desert	High Desertification

Forest	Tropical Deforestation	Polluted Water	Other Land

Human Pressure   Animals at Risk

Animal Pressure   Birds at Risk

0   200   400 miles

As the major source of the world's oil, the area is inevitably prone to serious pollution hazards. Tanker discharges at sea, high-technology wars, and deliberate sabotage have led to chaos in recent years.

Oil Pollution

Each year between 3 and 4 million tons of oil are released into the seas and oceans of the world. Consequences of major oil spills can be catastrophic. In 1978 oil spilled from *Amoco Cadiz,* polluting many miles of shoreline in northern France.

The most important source of oil entering the sea is released directly into rivers and oceans from urban and industrial areas. Over 1 million tons of oil a year enter the sea deliberately from ships, most of them oil tankers, as they wash out their empty tanks with sea water. This is illegal but the practice is still common. Soon satellite monitoring will be able to identify offenders and fine them when the tanker returns to port.

About half of the floating oil that pollutes the world's oceans is in the Mediterranean. The refineries and loading terminals of northern Libya make the Gulf of Sidra one of the most heavily polluted parts of the Mediterranean. This pollution has killed many spiny lobsters off Tunisia and Turkey. The breeding grounds of mackerel have also been seriously affected.

Sources of oil pollution each year

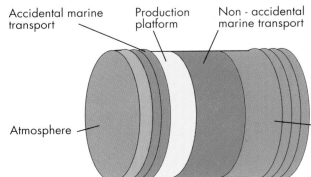

Accidental marine transport
Production platform
Non - accidental marine transport
Atmosphere
Urban and industrial

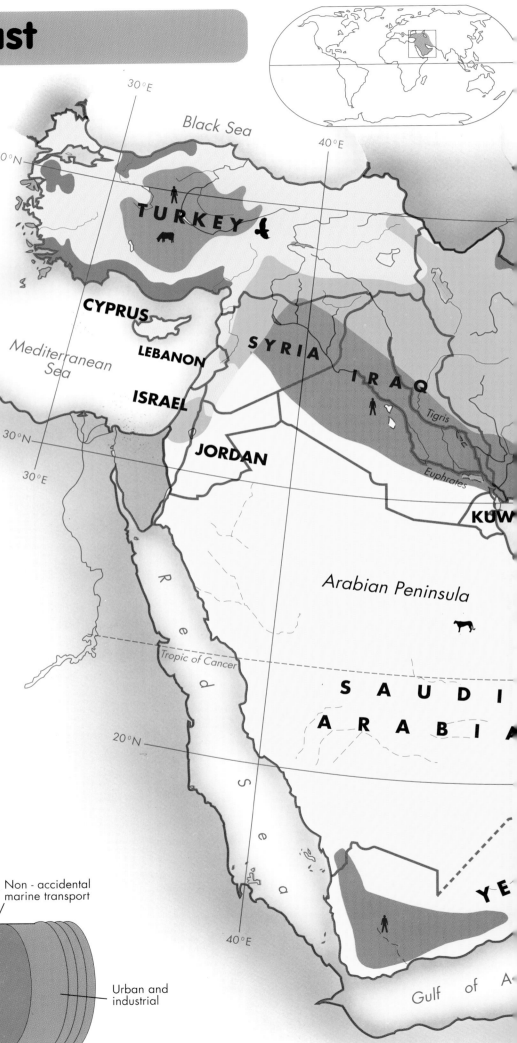

Endangered Corner

Arabian Onyx — once could be found over much of the Arabian Peninsula because it can survive in desert conditions. Thought to be extinct in the wild, over 200 Arabian onyx are kept in captive herds in Saudi Arabia and in zoos.

Cleaning Up an Oil Slick

1. Leave it: let it break up naturally if it is a long way from land. Satellite monitoring is used to keep a watch on it. Eventually it will disappear, though sticky tar balls will appear around the coastline months later.
2. Dispersants: strong detergents can be used on the oil to break it up more quickly; however these chemicals kill marine life, so they cannot be used too near the shoreline.
3. Sinking: oil can be made to sink to the ocean floor by spreading powdered chalk on it. While this clears the surface, the sea bed is still damaged.
4. Absorption: materials such as straw, peat, and polystyrene can absorb the oil and then be collected.
5. Booms: floating barriers can be used to contain the oil slick and stop it spreading onto a beach. The oil can then be sucked up by tankers.

Water used per person
1985 – 1988

Turkey

= 250 gallons

= 125 gallons

Caspian Sea

I R A N

BAHRAIN

QATAR

UNITED ARAB EMIRATES

Arabian Sea

O M A N

60°E

40°N

30°N

Tropic of Cancer

20°N

60°E

Forests Lost

Turkey

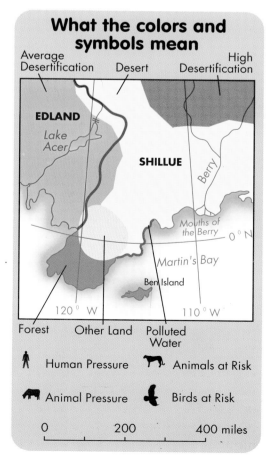

What the colors and symbols mean

Average Desertification   Desert   High Desertification

EDLAND

Lake Acer

SHILLUE

Berry

Mouths of the Berry   0° N

Martin's Bay

Ben Island

120° W   110° W

Forest   Other Land   Polluted Water

Human Pressure   Animals at Risk

Animal Pressure   Birds at Risk

0   200   400 miles

Intelligent and social, the dolphin is at ever-increasing risk from mankind. Modern high-volume fishing methods account for many unnecessary deaths of this popular species, and exploitation in aquaria is being discouraged.

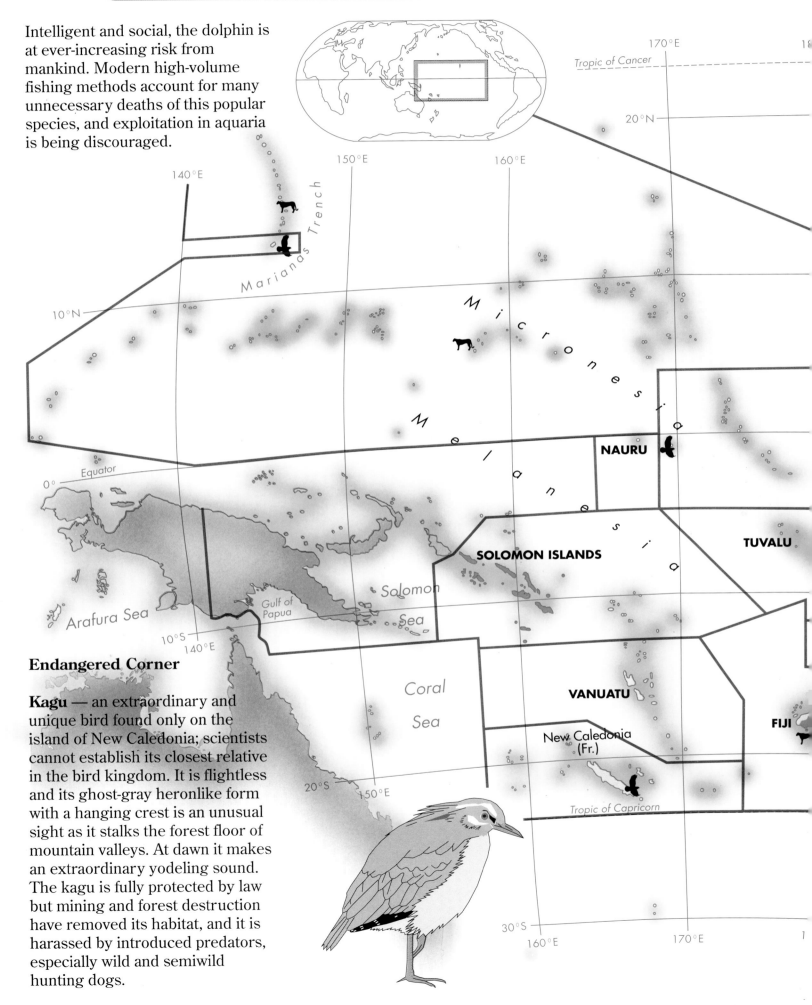

Endangered Corner

Kagu — an extraordinary and unique bird found only on the island of New Caledonia; scientists cannot establish its closest relative in the bird kingdom. It is flightless and its ghost-gray heronlike form with a hanging crest is an unusual sight as it stalks the forest floor of mountain valleys. At dawn it makes an extraordinary yodeling sound. The kagu is fully protected by law but mining and forest destruction have removed its habitat, and it is harassed by introduced predators, especially wild and semiwild hunting dogs.

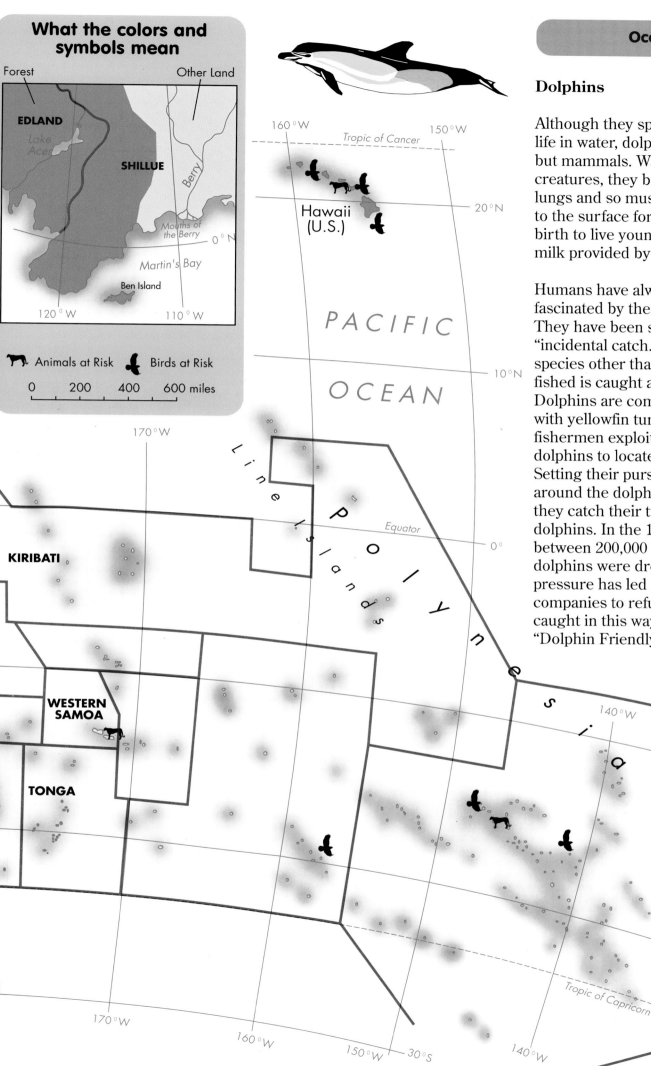

What the colors and symbols mean

Forest

Other Land

EDLAND

Lake Acer

SHILLUE

Berry

Mouths of the Berry

0°N

Martin's Bay

Ben Island

120°W   110°W

🐎 Animals at Risk   🦅 Birds at Risk

0   200   400   600 miles

Dolphins

Although they spend their entire life in water, dolphins are not fish but mammals. Warm-blooded creatures, they breathe air with lungs and so must periodically rise to the surface for air. They give birth to live young that suckle on milk provided by the mother.

Humans have always been fascinated by the sociable dophins. They have been subject to "incidental catch." This is when a species other than the one being fished is caught and killed. Dolphins are commonly associated with yellowfin tuna, and the fishermen exploit sightings of dolphins to locate shoals of tuna. Setting their purse-seine nets around the dolphin-tuna school, they catch their tuna but drown the dolphins. In the 1960s and 1970s between 200,000 and 500,000 dolphins were drowned. Consumer pressure has led many big companies to refuse to buy tuna caught in this way. Look for "Dolphin Friendly" on the tuna can.

160°W   Tropic of Cancer   150°W

Hawaii (U.S.)   20°N

10°N

PACIFIC

OCEAN

170°W

Line Islands

Equator   0°

KIRIBATI

Polynesia

WESTERN SAMOA

140°W

130°W

TONGA

10°S

20°S

Tropic of Capricorn   130°W

170°W   160°W   150°W   30°S   140°W

A land of wealthy consumers, the United States paid the price for overfarming in the Midwest with the "Dust Bowl," and U.S. imports are still responsible for much of the world's overproduction.

Endangered Corner

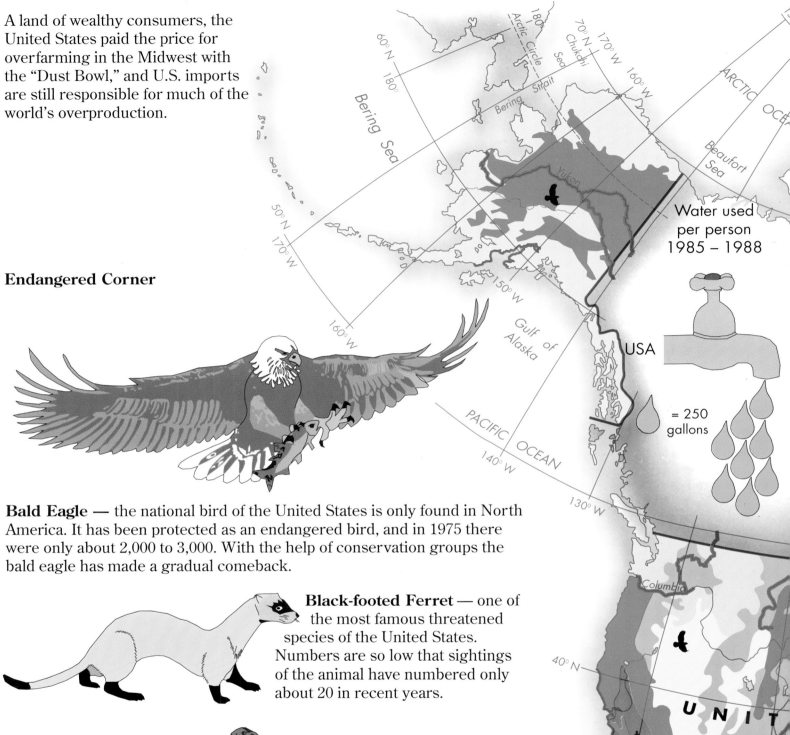

Water used per person 1985 – 1988

= 250 gallons

Bald Eagle — the national bird of the United States is only found in North America. It has been protected as an endangered bird, and in 1975 there were only about 2,000 to 3,000. With the help of conservation groups the bald eagle has made a gradual comeback.

Black-footed Ferret — one of the most famous threatened species of the United States. Numbers are so low that sightings of the animal have numbered only about 20 in recent years.

California Condor — one of the world's most threatened birds is defeating all attempts to save it. The condor is found in southern California, where its numbers have been declining for many years.

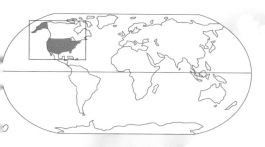

Wind Erosion

Dry regions that are intensely farmed suffer from wind erosion. The prairies of North America and the wheat-growing regions of the Ukraine and the steppes of the Kazakhstan in the former Soviet Union are two such areas. When vegetation is removed, forests cut down, or land overgrazed, the earth is exposed to the sun, and it quickly dries and crumbles. The wind picks up the dried earth and scatters it widely in dense clouds.

American Dust Bowl

One of the worst wind erosion disasters was in the 1930s, when American farmers using new methods tilled the Great Plains of Colorado, Kansas, New Mexico, Texas, and Oklahoma. Americans knew that something catastophic had happened when they had an unexpected partial eclipse of the sun.

It was in fact a giant dust cloud containing an estimated 355 million tons of fertile topsoil that had blown off the overcultivated and drought-ridden plains. The cloud blew as far as the East Coast, darkening Washington and New York, before depositing its contents into the sea. What was left was a vast bowl of potential desert that has taken 50 years to reclaim.

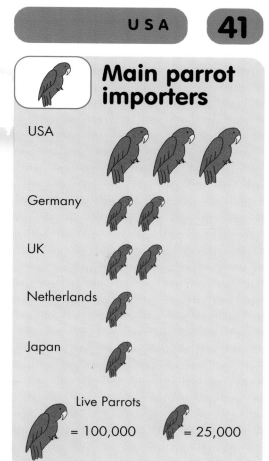

Main parrot importers

USA

Germany

UK

Netherlands

Japan

Live Parrots

= 100,000   = 25,000

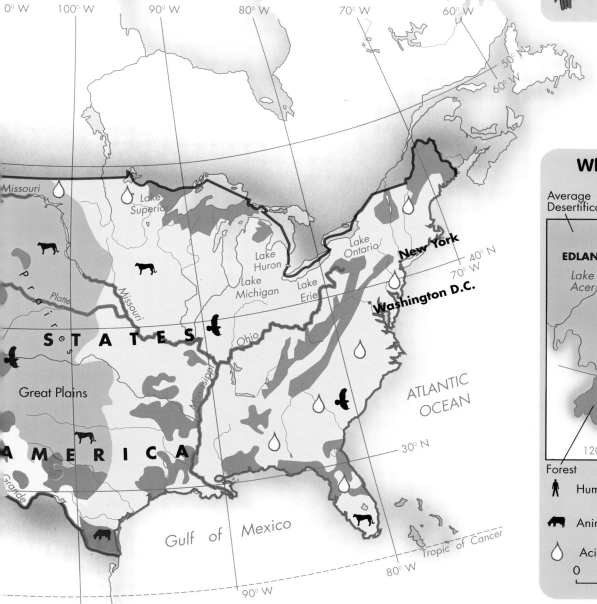

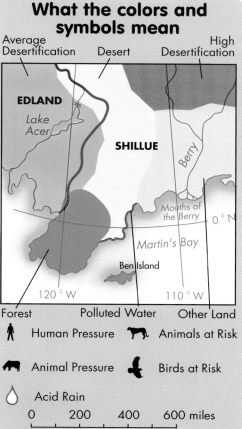

What the colors and symbols mean

Average Desertification   Desert   High Desertification

EDLAND

Lake Acer

SHILLUE

Berry

Mouths of the Berry

Martin's Bay

Ben Island

120° W   110° W

Forest   Polluted Water   Other Land

👤 Human Pressure   🐂 Animals at Risk

🐃 Animal Pressure   Birds at Risk

💧 Acid Rain

0   200   400   600 miles

Acid Rain
Rain that has been acidified as it descends from the clouds, picking up pollutants from the atmosphere.

Biodegradable
Capable of being decomposed by bacteria or other biological means.

Browsing
Feeding on vegetation by constant nibbling.

Conservation
Protection, preservation, and careful management of natural resources.

Decomposition
To rot or breakdown into basic elements through bacterial or fungal action.

Ecology
The science that studies living organisms in relation to their environment.

Ecosystem
A community of plants and animals and their immediate environment, including the nonliving environment.

Erosion
The wearing away of land surface by various natural agencies, including wind, sea, rivers, and rain.

Fossil fuel
Naturally occurring fuel such as coal, gas, and oil, formed by decomposition of living organisms.

Habitat
The natural environment of a plant or animal.

Holocaust
Great destruction or loss of life.

Molluscs
A group of invertebrates with soft unsegmented bodies and shells. They include snails, clams and mussels, cuttlefish, and octopuses.

Mutation
A change in the chromosomes or genes of a cell that effects the structure and development of the resultant offspring.

Ozone layer
The part of the atmosphere that extends from about 6 miles to about 30 miles above the earth's surface and contains ozone, which shields the earth from ultraviolet radiation.

Parasite
An animal or plant that lives in or on another organism from which it gains its nourishment.

Plankton
Organisms inhabiting the surface layer of a sea or lake, consisting of small drifting plants and animals.

Purse seine net
A large fishing net that envelops fish and is then closed at the bottom by means of a line, rather like a purse string.

Recycling
Reclaiming something for further use.

Savannah
Open grasslands, usually with scattered bushes and trees.

Semi-arid
The climate of the regions on the fringe of the deserts where the rainfall is slightly higher and the vegetation a little less sparse than the deserts. Also called scrub.

Species
A group of animals or plants all sharing common attributes and capable of interbreeding; the subdivision of a genus.

Temperate area
A climate between the extremes of tropical and polar, enjoying distinct warm and cool seasons.

Tropics
The region between the Tropic of Cancer and the Tropic of Capricorn. The weather in general is always hot.

Volatility
The tendency to change rapidly and unexpectedly.

Anderson, Madelyn Klein. *Oil Spills.*
New York: Watts, 1990.

Ashworth, William. *Nor Any Drop To Drink.*
New York: Summit Books, 1982.

Baines, John D. *Acid Rain.*
Austin: Steck-Vaughn, 1990.

Baines, John D. *Protecting The Oceans.*
Austin: Steck-Vaughn, 1991.

Barss, Karen. *Clean Water.*
New York: Chelsea House, 1992.

Becklake, John. *Pollution.*
New York: Gloucester Press, 1990.

Cherrington, Mark. *Degradation of the Land.*
New York: Chelsea House, 1992.

Edelson, Edward. *Clean Air.*
New York: Chelsea House, 1992.

Gold, Susan Dudley. *Toxic Waste.*
New York: Crestwood House, 1990.

Woods, Geraldine. *Pollution.*
New York: Watts, 1985.

This index is designed to help you to find places shown on the maps. The index is in alphabetical order and lists all towns, countries, and physical features. After each entry extra information is given to describe the entry and to tell you which country or continent it is in.

The next column contains the latitude and longitude figures. These are used to help locate places on maps. They are measured in degrees. The blue lines drawn across the map are lines of latitude. The equator is at latitude 0°. All lines above the equator are referred to as °N (north of the equator). All lines below the equator are referred to as °S (south of the equator).

The blue lines drawn from the top to the bottom of the map are lines of longitude. The 0° line passes through Greenwich, London, and is known as the Greenwich Meridian. All lines of longitude join the North Pole to the South Pole. All lines to the right of the Greenwich Meridian are referred to as °E (east of Greenwich), and all lines to the left of the Greenwich Meridian are referred to as °W (west of Greenwich).

The final column indicates the number of the page where you will find the place for which you are searching.

If you want to find out where the Gulf of Thailand is, look it up in the alphabetical index. The entry will read:

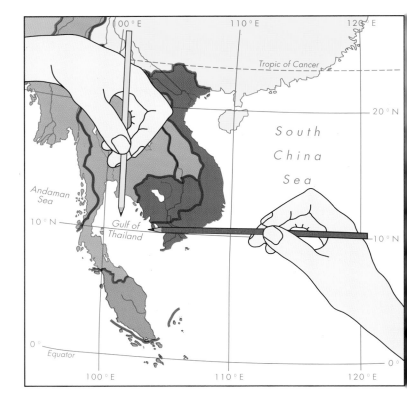

Name, Description	Location		Page
	Lat.	Long.	
Thailand, Gulf of, Asia	11°N	101°E	22

Turn to page 22 in your atlas. The Gulf of Thailand is located where latitude 11°N meets longitude 101°E. Place a pencil along latitude 11°N. Now take another pencil and place it along 101°E. Where the two pencils meet is the location of the Gulf of Thailand. Practice finding places in the index and on the maps.

Scott E. Morris is an associate professor of geography at the University of Idaho, where his current areas of teaching and research interest include mountain geomorphology, field methods, and human impact on the landscape process. Dr. Morris received his Ph.D. from the University of Colorado, Boulder, and has published prolifically on the formation and climatic history of mountain landscapes, the effects of wildfire and mineral resource extraction on soil erosion processes, and the influence of water diversion and channel modification on sediment transport.